RYCHKUN'S LAWS OF AQ'ISM

Exposing Corporations

by
Ed Rychkun

ISBN 978-0-9782623-9-6

Copyright © 2014 Ed Rychkun

This material was originally published by Ed Rychkun in 2004. All rights are reserved and The AQ Principle© is copyright. But if you feel it is necessary to let people know that they may be falling victim to the AQ virus, or they need a laugh, feel free to use the material or please refer them to my website at www.edrychkun.com. What I do ask, however, is that you simply provide a reference to me whenever and if ever you use the material.

TABLE OF CONTENTS

INTRODUCTION	4
1 RYCHKUN'S LAWS	13
2 AQ'ISM IN ACTION	24
3 MEASURING YOUR AQ	40
4 AQ AND YOUR PRODUCTIVITY	47
5 AQ DIS-EQUILIBRIUM	54
6 SO WHAT'S YOUR AQ?	55
7 SOME AQ EXAMPLES	70
Case 1: Scooter Blastoff	70
Case 2: Oscar Ostrich	71
Case 3: Eric Von Shithead	73
Case 4: Donna Dingdong	74
8 THE EXECUTIVES	76
The Business Of Meetings	76
What's The Big Deal About Meetings?	80
So What's The Secret?	81
The Corporate Playground or Battleground?	82
The Corporate Executive	87
The Great Transition	91
Boardroom Brawling	93
The Laws Of Executive Regression	94
The Six Executive Arsenals	97

INTRODUCTION

Before you read another sentence, I want you to understand clearly that this book is my own personal satire of the corporate world. It is my view of corporations stripped naked of their glamour and efficiency. When I look back at how I climbed the "ladder of success" to take on positions of CEO, Partner, Director, Owner and Chairman... all those supposedly respected positions, I realize there wasn't really a lot of things learned at University that helped me get there. Perhaps I was lucky but I think perhaps I learned some things that were just not taught in school. What became apparent in the climb was what I saw as the "underbelly" of a corporation and a certain behavior in successful people that went far outside of the normal MBA training. What was so interesting to me was that there was a huge textbook of unwritten material on how people actually succeed to power and position in a corporation without following the traditional management stuff.

This book is where I bring this unwritten material to you. It strips companies of their usual look and practices thereby revealing the underbelly. When you look at your company and your experience in this light, I hope that you will get many chuckles and perhaps a different perspective on your journey upwards in the company.

I first began this book in 1986 after spending many years engaging in what many people call climbing the professional ladder. My parents were particularly poor so they spent a lot of time convincing me to go to school so I didn't have to be poor like them. Like a good lad, I set my journey towards corporate life in the business world... with absolutely no idea what I was headed for. My entry into business was fairly easy as I had worked part time through university. This business world I was peeking into looked so rewarding. After all, it was the place to be. It was after graduating from university, however, that I really got immersed in this folly. And I got the bug like many others! It seemed that no matter where I was or what I was doing, there was always someone smarter, more powerful, and wealthier than me. There were also more people that seemed pretty stupid with power as well. But through my "educated" glasses it was those guys that were better than me that I needed to follow, so I began to climb in an effort to be like them. It was only logical that I should climb up the same corporate ladder that they climbed. After all, it got these guys what many strived for... more power and money.

So I climbed for some thirty years. What a struggle! Some years were great. Others were horrible. But with conviction I worked and worked, followed the rules and slowly transformed myself from technical positions in the information industry up into supervisory roles and then into management. Basically, I just followed others, took management courses and worked as hard as I could. I never questioned the process. But I noticed that not everyone worked as hard as me. Some of the guys with power and money seemed like such jerks. They didn't even seem to know what they were talking about. Yet they were feared and respected by the others... plus they made a lot of money. Was I missing something?

Then, somewhere along the journey, I got to know the breed of corporate people called the "executive". These were always the golden guys that we all admired. What was so interesting about so many of these guys was that they seemed to work hard but they didn't really work... everybody else did. Was I doing something wrong? Did I go to the wrong training program? What was it that I was missing? It was only when I started to attend management and executive meetings that the secret started to reveal itself. It became apparent that many of these top leaders of corporations used many unwritten tactics to control and manipulate people. Oh yes, I will admit there are exceptions but I didn't meet many.

As I ascended the corporate ladders, I began to develop a rather oblique humorous perspective of the business world and these corporate leaders. It was here that I began to materialize a hypothesis that I dubbed as the AQ Phenomenon. Very much like the process called the "Peter Principal", the *AQ process defined how and why so many people get into disharmony with their fellow employees and how and why, despite the conflict, some still rise in status while so many others failed.* It was at that time, as Director of Information Services, that I was beginning to question my sanity and I began to look at things in a different light. The whole process of growth, promotion, career became fuzzy as I began to see conflict with the kind of person I really was. Knowing that I would have to change my personality, levels of aggression, social sphere of influence and many other individual traits if I wanted to rise farther became somewhat disconcerting. Sometimes I had to fire people, even humiliate them because they did not follow directives or rules. Sometimes I was even told by a superior that I had to treat people more horribly. What was becoming bothersome was that, as a survival tactic, I was expected to treat others like assholes or they would destroy my credibility. Even more troublesome was my changing perception of certain people in the company, and my respect for them, never mind my potential relationship with them. It was difficult to understand why so many of these people had so much power and position entrusted to them when they were really such awful jerks.

It was difficult to see how I could be part of this peculiar culture. What I observed and felt, I began to quantify in this rather obtuse process I called AQ. As I began to reflect and write about my findings I decided that I needed to get out into a new job. I decided to move to Africa and took a senior position in a new area with IBM in South Africa. You can imagine the shock. This time it took me only two years to reach another level of awareness and one of conflict with myself. The picture of what was happening was clearer now, one that allowed me to complete yet another chapter in this book. But there was still something missing... I didn't feel I had climbed high enough in the business world to give credence to my theories. So the book sat in limbo while I climbed higher in the corporate tree.

In 1988, I returned to Canada to take a Vice President position with a high tech company and truthfully forgot about my scribbling. After I became President in 1989 I began to view my interaction with people from a new level and revisited my theories, completing another chapter. When I finally gave up this position in 1997 as it was time to get out on my own as a Financial Consultant, Author and Entrepreneur. I decided to move into those positions in a quest to be free and get to a situation where no one could tell me what to do and work in my own free enterprise system. But it wasn't long before I hitched up with new partners. After being part Founder, Director, and CFO of a Private Bank in the Caribbean, then CFO of an Investment Fund Company, I realized that my hypothesis on AQ was even more relevant at the top of the heap. It didn't seem to matter what position I took, I was beholding to clients, shareholders, directors and even partners and govern-governments who could get on my AQ list when the boom and bust cycles occurred.

Now don't get me wrong... I didn't go higher just to write a book, the idea was to attain more freedom. But this is where I became familiar with some new titles like founder, partner, director, chairman.... and so ends the story. That's where it all stopped. I could then report that I had climbed through every major step in the corporate world and beyond. In 2002, I decided it was time to share my findings and begin writing about this.

What I had determined was that employees, regardless of position, exhibit certain behaviors and characteristics that are anything but "professional". I discovered that the word organization was really a myth. The word management was really an invisible ability to collect a bunch of untaught techniques to manipulate others. I discovered that the rate of progression (or regression) in a company was actually dependant on something unexpected. The progression related to how you relate to others in the company... and more important... how you feel about them.

The whole phenomenon is wrapped up in your AQ, short for "Asshole Quotient". This is simply a measurement of your relationship to others in the company. The reality was that just about everyone in a corporation kept a secret mental list. This list contained people that they had determined were jerks... more aggressively referred to as "assholes". It is how big (or small) an individual list is relative to the individual's position in the corporation that is the crucial concern. Sound silly? Well first, let me warn you. If you are not endowed with a sense of humor about your job, or you have difficulty seeing anything amusing about corporate life, then you may not want to read this book. It may even depress you further when you realize how ridiculous we are.

Anyone who has lived in the corporate world, and I mean anyone who has worked in some organizational structure, will understand the need to grow as a professional citizen. It becomes apparent quite early in anyone's career that many traumatic experiences will be found along the way. Whether the pathway leads upwards or sideways seems to matter very little, for in either case, various rules and regulations, policies and procedures, cultures and personalities, will be encountered. These, sooner or later, will lead to disagreement or conflict. This process inevitably adds more people to the secret list. What becomes apparent is that this list is actually very important in determining how you succeed or fail in an organization. The use of this secret list is what the AQ is all about.

It is this culture, and the way companies work that is the topic here... but with a different slant than management books. Call this one "un-management" if you will... it is a look at the silly but true underbelly of a corporation. That's why I call it "Corporations Stripped Naked".

What you will read about is anything but orderly management and organizational efficiency. Rather, you will get a picture of the flip side of a company and its people. The AQ phenomenon is universal. It reveals the untaught secrets of those "successful" executives and managers. The material will vary from serious treatments to satire and exaggeration. It will inject raw humor into the grim realities of corporate life.

Special thanks are given to those many assholes I met from the past. I have met many and you are also about to meet them in this book. Some are purposely exaggerated to make a point. Thanks to them, they have made this book possible.

There is a final note here and it came about when I began to promote the book. On many interviews, after describing the AQ process, people would ask for advice on how to deal with their problems at work. This was not the intent. It was to show how people become "***Corporites***" that acquire the AQ Virus that sucks us into the mire of corporate power and need to use or abuse others. It stems from a need to preserve the ego and to protect one's position. It is something that happens to people when they engage in this Corporite addiction which is like ***corporitis***, the power and preservation addiction of a very contagious virus which I call **AQ'ISM.**

Once this virus takes hold you begin to lose your real personality and it becomes a ***corporitic*** need to survive. At the extreme, corporitis renders a company dysfunctional in what I call AQ-disequilibrium where everybody thinks everybody else is an asshole and the level of productivity (and service) infects the balance sheet, and even clients believe the company is full of assholes. That is usually bankruptcy, and I have experienced those as well.

As it turns out, to be corporitic, you need to be a dead human, like what the Corporation itself is - a dead entity for the sole purpose of engaging in commerce usually for a profit - which is without emotion or a conscience. Typically we call those beings in a corporation Assholes but it is because corporations become profitable and grow because of a dependence and interdependence on their employees. and that is where the way we do this -

with or without emotion - make the big difference as to how the AQ Virus has taken hold.

This book is meant to show how employees typically take on this virus and how they shift in their corporitic behavior to become Assholes in other corporite citizens.

The big lesson here is **not** how to teach you to become an asshole addicted by ego preservation and desire for power. It is to see how the AQ Virus is caught, its symptoms, it's common behavior patterns, and to have laugh so as to avoid losing your good side of emotion and happy interrelationship in your job.

The book will refer to many of these behavior patterns as tools. I have observed these as common habits when one gets the virus. Of course to the one addicted to the power over people and the need to protect money and ego, these are tools that they use perhaps unknowingly, just like an alcoholic or smoker is unknowingly addicted to the habit.

And so, please do not seek advice on this. It is all to open your heart and avoid the AQ Virus so **you do not become** a Corporate Zombie that uses and abuses others for the sake of egoist pride and the insatiable urge to attain power over others through commerce.

When I got to the top, I found that my basic constitution was having a bad time of treating people under the spell of the virus always being ruthlessly conscious of profit, and covering my ass. I was copying what I thought was a successful formula as exhibited by the majority of corporate leaders that eventually gave me heartache and heartburn.

That's why I had to exit the corporite addiction of AQ'ISM and retrench my habits.

At some point, when this happens, you need to make some serious changes to carve out a different "corporate" path.

There are always choices in these dead corporations; to engage others in a good way or a bad way. Once you see the folly of the AQ Virus, what will you choose?

This is an abridged version of the Laws. For a full treatment of the Arsenals and a truly naked corporation, please go to my books:

Corporations Stripped Naked 1: Exposing The AQ Virus
Corporations Stripped Naked 2: Controlling The AQ Virus
Found at Amazon.com

and

www.edrychkun.com

Ed Rychkun

1 RYCHKUN'S LAWS

When people join corporate structures, they must obviously learn rules, policies and procedures. They must also meet new people who begin to influence their habits and activities. Some are nice. Some are jerks. Some are smart, and some are not. Others are incompetent, while some are professional. This results in a progression where some fail badly while others succeed. Yet progression in the company seems to have little relationship to these new people's traits regardless of whether they are bad or good. For many, it becomes a mystery how they are judged. How is it that some never get promoted? How is it that some become Presidents while others remain at the bottom? How come some VP's are absolute incompetent jerks and they are still respected? What is this mysterious decision process that these corporate cultures keep within their walls?

At the base of all this is a strange culture that has people randomly failing and succeeding. There is a preoccupation with profit or some measurable means of results... a corporate performance yardstick. It is this performance yardstick and your relationship to it that has a dramatic impact on how you feel about others in the corporation.

It becomes apparent quite early in anyone's career that many traumatic experiences will be found along the way, depending on how much you contribute to the profit culture, or how well you adjust to the power hierarchy and how you measure up to this yardstick. Wherever your professional progress leads, you will always be subjected to the various rules and regulations, policies and procedures, cultures and personalities that will mystify you. These, sooner or later, will lead to "joining the fold" or "falling from the fold" and you will form an opinion about the ones that have affected you... or measured you.

Out of this process has been born a universal phenomenon that creates a preoccupation with the word asshole. Whenever a citizen disagrees with another citizen, he is quite likely to refer to him as an asshole. He can be a big one, a stupid one or a disgusting one. This relates to the size or degree. In addition, it is difficult, no matter where you are, or who you are, to at some time in your corporate career, resist the temptation of saying or thinking that disgusting word.

You may be surprised to know that you are not alone. This particular term is more universal than you can ever imagine. It is, after all, a rather effective quantification of someone else. And in its use, it happens to actually reflect the fundamental behavior and attitudes of the corporate citizens that you are trying to describe in one word... does it not? If you really look at how it is applied, it describes a universal characteristic of anyone whether a junior worker or a president.

Everyone uses the term *asshole*, some just think it, others say it. Have you ever thought "what an asshole"? And how many times have you wanted to say: "My, my, you are a big asshole"? Yes it's crude... but oh so descriptive! This word, and how you use it, say it, think it, quantifies how you feel about, and deal with, other people in the company. It even reflects how you treat them or how you deal with them. And it also reflects how they feel about you. So now you come to the crux of the matter. An AQ is as quantifiable as an IQ, but much, much more revealing as you shall learn shortly.

So here is the crux. Within corporate walls, in virtually every space, there are people called employees who will, for some peculiar reason, eventually refer to each other as "assholes". Either in thought, actions, conversations, or through more esoteric communications, this colloquial terminology is eventually included in a corporate citizen's conscious space and vocabulary. Believe it or not, this is a universal habit. This preoccupation with the human posterior is not easily explained - let it be sufficient to say that it has evolved as a fairly common mental representation of someone else's qualities. This appears to be rooted in an association with some disgusting or disagreeable characteristics that the human posterior bears to someone you dislike or find disagreement with. This disagreement is, in any company, the basis for a strange phenomenon I call **AQ'ISM**. Believe it or not, even the most tight-lipped prude or the prettiest Miss Prim and Proper will eventually consider, and even utter, the word Asshole. Just ponder a while and think about how many times you've heard this expression... or may have even thought it of a fellow employee yourself? So now we have the meaning of the letter **A** in **AQ**.

Thus, when any corporate person is considered an asshole by another corporate citizen, it means that through some manner brought about by the corporate social or work mechanism, one person disagrees with, dislikes, or treats badly another within the same company.

Needless to say, the longer one associates with the same people, the more likely he or she is to become victim to this phenomenon. And quite clearly, it matters not how much one dislikes or disagrees with another, it only matters that an "asshole transformation" has occurred. Once this transformation occurs it is likely to stay. In fact, after the transformation occurs, one is likely to only add to the intensity, frequency of thought or the degree of asshole, eventually breaking down tolerance and efficiency - as we shall soon see. It is this transformation process that leads us to the concept of AQ'ISM.

AQ is short for **A**sshole **Q**uotient, which is simply the percentage of corporate citizens that any one person has converted to assholes. An AQ is therefore a personal measurement that will obviously vary from 0 (no Assholes and everybody is really nice) to 100 (everybody is an asshole - including yourself). In any company, there are a finite number of corporate citizens. For any one person, at any point in time, there will be some number of those citizens that he/she places on the asshole status list. The measurement of this state is one's AQ. It will be shown that AQ's will start at zero and increase with time - that they rarely decrease.

In general there appears to be three main interactive levels that reflect three different corporate divisions. These corporate divisions are Local (departmental), Divisional (operation, division or branch) and Corporate (head office). There appears also to be a very delicate balance between one's AQ level and one's position within these corporate groups (AQ Equilibrium).

The most interesting is the Head Office or Corporate AQ. It is this AQ and the Head Office culture that we will explore in the following chapters. Before proceeding, however, let us define some fundamental laws of AQ'ISM:

1st BASIC LAW OF AQ'ISM
There exists a natural tendency within any one corporation for any one individual to classify another as an Asshole.

2nd LAW OF AQ'ISM
The percent of Assholes within any company, as viewed by any one individual at any point in time, is defined as one's Asshole Quotient or "AQ" level.

Now let us look more closely at the AQ'ISM phenomenon. When any professional or career oriented individual joins a company, his or her association with other members of the "corporate family" is minimal to non-existent. It is, in fact, quite likely that a new employee, partner or associate will be impressed with the others, otherwise joining the group would not be considered. Although exceptions may arise, for the most part, the initial contact and association is either neutral or positive. So in one's narrow little sphere, one's AQ is simply zero.... everyone is very nice, professional, smart, etc., etc.

But that sphere soon begins to grow. And, since one of the main objectives is to get along with and impress others so that one's career and subsequent rewards grow, one inevitably begins to deal with others at a more detailed level. As one settles into the company and the position, the association with others begins to broaden, as may the nature of the work. Typically one may become involved in meetings, gatherings, services, projects, verbal exchanges, or social events. Consequently, one is exposed to, and gains impressions of other's ideas, habits, opinions, capabilities and so forth. As this process continues, a person begins to phase from impressions to conclusions. As these take on a contrary nature, the result, that is one's opinion, may vary. Acceptance is a start but soon enough it may be tolerance. Or maybe disagreement prevails, perhaps even outright aggression. That is, the more one becomes exposed to other people and their ideas, the greater is the potential for disagreement.

If one gets too much of this too fast the results can be serious aggression or even depression. This has a tendency to create side effects in the form of discontentment or dissatisfaction, both of which can be recognized by others who may start to form their own opinion of the new recruit. Thus, as time ticks on, from the day of entry, as relationships, job exposure and job demands broaden, there will be a natural tendency to move new people into one's personal asshole list. Similarly, others in the company also form an impression of a new employee and, and given sufficient time, they eventually convert that person into an asshole. This conversion process whereby each can mentally convert the other is called **Interassholism**. It has some grave consequences that will be dealt with later.

In any case, consider a chronology of statements over time. It illustrates the AQ process. Imagine Barry Brass who just took a new job. These are his thoughts as he progresses in his employment:

"I took the job because of new opportunities and because the company is professional. I am impressed with the people."

"The amount of material in this report from Sam is unreal - was it all necessary?"

"Those three idiots in the information technology division sure are stupid."

"The office services division should be called office disservices - why doesn't the manager see how poor the service is and fire those four smart-ass typists?"

"These policies are absurd. Can't these two people realize the obvious benefits without this crap."

"The people responsible are twits - how can you get new ideas across to these two imbeciles."

"How can this Asshole give me such a poor performance review when I worked so much overtime?"

You will notice Barry's increasing aggressive and changing attitude, along with his increasing AQ. Not only is his AQ rising, so is his exposure and profile. Barry eventually converted his boss into asshole status... a fairly serious problem. Now let's look at some thoughts and statements from Barry's boss through the same period of time:

"I just hired this guy Barry Brass. He has a degree in Engineering and is as sharp as a razor - I expect him to be my right hand man."

"Barry, your evaluation of the report was quite well done but the comments on the amount of redundant information wasn't appreciated by the author."

"I will have to go down to the information technology division and tell the group that Barry was just

in a bad mood - too much pressure - he didn't really mean to call the R&D group bearded weirdoes."

"Barry, why didn't you talk to me before you sent that memo about the smart-ass typists?"

"These policies may be crap, but this does not mean that you can ignore a justification procedure. I suggest that you do a proper write up."

"You must do it that way, Mr. Brass, simply because I said so."

"Yes sir, I will speak with Barry, I don't think he meant to call you twits at the meeting."

"Barry, we have decided to give you no salary increase until you change your poor attitude..."

"How do I get rid of this asshole before he causes me any more trouble?"

But this is not the whole picture. There is a third side to this problem. The rest of the company that Barry is slowly getting to know is also involved in the AQ story. Some of the other people involved in Barry's corporate family are also placing him on their own AQ lists. Here are some more thoughts throughout the same period of time:

"We met Barry at the company picnic, he certainly seems to be on the ball."

"Where does this Brass kid get off telling me to take a course in writing?"

"The next time Mr. Brass excites my people this way we will have to settle the problem at the VP level."

"My wife and I met Mr. Brass at the party - he sure is a smart-ass.

"You know that scum bag Brass told me I should learn how to type as fast as I gossip."

"If we don't watch out for this Brass guy we might jeopardize the project."

So Barry went merrily along slowly converting people to assholes. Not too surprising is that, given Barry's changing attitude, the boss and some other people were also converting Barry to the same status. What was happening was that Barry's AQ was rising. He started at zero and began to work diligently at increasing it over time. Now we can construct a few more simple laws.

3rd LAW OF AQ'ISM
Any new entry into a corporation will tend to have an individual AQ near zero.

4th LAW OF AQ'ISM
Any individual AQ, given sufficient time, will tend towards 100.

5th LAW OF AQ'ISM
Individual AQ's have a tendency to rise according to a natural growth process.

6th LAW OF AQ'ISM
From the date of entry into a corporation, an individual carefully sets out to prove that he or she is an Asshole.

7th LAW OF AQ'ISM
Sooner or later any individual will freely offer evidence to prove that he or she is an Asshole.

Well what does this mean? It means that people are constantly working towards becoming assholes and improving their own AQ'S. It is a natural tendency.

In further studying the AQ phenomenon, particularly as it changes in time, certain interesting observations can be made. It follows that if too many people think you are an asshole your job may be in jeopardy - you are reaching a dangerous external AQ level. Similarly, if you think too many people are assholes, *you* can approach a dangerous AQ level. Obviously, given sufficient time, your actions and opinions will become more overt. This may cause a conflict that jeopardizes your job. Although there is no hard fast rule as to what the danger level is, it is safe to say that once you reach certain levels beyond your corporate allocation, you could be in trouble and certain precautions may become necessary. This will, of course, depend upon how many immediate "bosses" are on your list and what your corporate position is. The individual allocation, called the AQ Equilibrium, will become clear later.

8th LAW OF AQ'ISM
AQ's have a tendency to be reciprocal in motion.

When someone considers you an asshole, it is likely that you will feel or hear this and you feel likewise, or even stronger, about that person. This reciprocal AQ action was illustrated in the case of Barry Brass. Effectively, this process can cause assholes to be created in a chain reaction effect where one can get on someone else's AQ list without even knowing it.

Thus the AQ laws are always at work in a company of people. The fundamentals of AQ'ISM are indeed simple - just a process of converting each other to assholes. Now that we have the basics, simply think about the people you know and work with. How would you rate your AQ today?

Ok, before we move on, here is something you need to really think about when relating to the AQ process. When you first join a corporation you love everybody, right? Well, you will encounter someone who may put you off... so you may **think** that this person is an asshole. But conflicts are inevitable. If someone really puts you off or says something nasty, you may even **infer** that this person is an asshole to someone else. At some point you may let your frustrations out and **call** someone an asshole indirectly. Actually, you may find that you do not usually attain a supervisory role unless you have the "moxy" to **call** someone else an asshole. The transition to manager may actually require that you confront people directly to **tell** them they are an asshole. The next level can only be achieved by being able to **treat** others as assholes if this becomes necessary in the course of duty.

Now you are ready to see how this works in a real case.

2 AQ'ISM IN ACTION

Should one study the career path of many individuals, it would be easy to see that they start somewhere in some junior position in the company. This is the first level. After some time they would attain more responsibilities and possibly some independence. In further progressing, they may deal with others outside the immediate area. They could even gain more responsibility and gain authority over others, depending upon "performance".

Similarly, the second level called management, could be achieved when new corporate players became exposed to them and judge their performance on a wider basis. The entry into the third, executive, level, would again be based upon performance with higher or more far reaching responsibilities. Moving from the bottom to the top of this pyramid requires successful movement through a corporate hierarchy through hard work and consistent performance centered at improving all that is the company. Or does it really work this way? Let us examine the AQ process and its relation to the three levels.

Wherever you go, or wherever you are, whether in a simple company with one office or a multinational with large corporations scattered about the world, there are three main structures... executives, management and the rest. Regardless of size, some pyramid structure exists - only the titles and reporting structure becomes more complex.

Thus there are three groups of people synonymous with the structure in the pyramid. There is always movement through this structure as players attempt to progress from the "lower reaches" to trample, grope and climb towards the "upper echelon".

What is significant to the AQ process is its behavior in any physical group within the overall corporate structure. This could be a head office, an operation branch, sub-office, or whatever. Each group will usually include the three levels of people, mainly the executive, middle management and the workers.

As it turns out, there are also three similar AQ levels to be aware of that correspond to position. As your AQ rises, so can your position in the pyramid. First let us look at a company called STEADFAST MEATS LTD and the AQ process as one individual Franklin P. Hardass climbs his way to the top of the pyramid. What you will see happening is a strange metamorphic process as he moves upwards.

Franklin P. Hardass is now the President and Chief Executive Officer of a large meatpacking and distribution company. He sits comfortably at the top of the pyramid in the "Upper Echelon". It took poor Frank 20 years to work his way up from the very bottom of the "Lower Reaches". He started his career when he was back in high school working in the slaughterhouse oiling mechanical equipment... not a particularly pleasant job but in those days, who could be picky?

Quite normally, when Frank started, his AQ was zero... he thought that everybody was great... the 3rd Law. All the people were hard working and he was learning incredible things from them. It was great to have a job and be part of this fantastic company and competent team. There wasn't a soul that he could say anything bad about. Frank was a fairly fast kid so it wasn't long before he learned his job fairly well, became used to his responsibilities and started to change. Frank unknowingly was to become victim to AQ'ISM. He began to notice that some of his co-workers liked to sluff off whenever possible. This started out being somewhat funny as he watched them devise ways to avoid work but it took on a more serious air when some of the slacking had a direct effect on Frank. Frank was dedicated. He did not want it to look like he was also part of this slacker's conspiracy.

Frank just worked harder and oiled more thoroughly to cover his mumblings and to cover for them. Several things were happening. Frank was changing his opinion of his co-workers. He was now bewildered about his boss being so stupid about the obvious infractions. The Basic Law of AQ'ISM was beginning to have its effect. In the meantime the co-workers began to wonder about Frank... who could be seen working after the shift to make things work. Frank and the co-workers, independently began to think about each other as not so cool... "assholes" so to speak. The reciprocal AQ Law Number 7 was now working.

Not too unpredictably, Frank's local AQ began to rise as the situation continued. Even though he didn't say too much, he began to convert his co-workers into a bunch of assholes. So far, Frank was a bit apprehensive to say anything for fear that he would get someone annoyed at him so his grumbling velocity increased.

As it turns out, Frank was learning loads of new stuff from his Mechanical Engineering course. He began to pay more attention to some of the activities surrounding the equipment. He noted that some of the co-workers must have lost all their marbles to be doing some of the things he saw. And some actually got hurt and couldn't come to work. Then Frank did something new. He suggested to some that they were a bit stupid - that they should watch the equipment. Now Frank was operating under Law 5. He wasn't just **thinking** that they were assholes, he was beginning to **infer** that they were assholes. He suggested that they should watch the equipment more carefully and move in only when the large mechanical arm retracted - this would save the company time and money, he said. Well this time Frank just annoyed more of the other workers - who the hell did this oiler think he was - telling people how to do their job? Frank finally went to his boss and told him that he had some ideas that would improve

the efficiency of the equipment and work place. It might even get rid of some of those "useless assholes" as he called them.

Since the boss was a bit of a wimp when it came to dealing with people, Frank's suggestions were an opportunity to delegate, so he put Frank in charge of the oilers and set up a special project to try out the ideas. Well, needless to say, Frank now had to tell a few oilers to "get their stuff together" or "hit the road". Frank's AQ was rising. He was now **telling** people they were Assholes.

And Frank's device worked. He realigned the arm and lifted it out of the way, making it less dangerous and improving its speed. This process not only improved the mechanism, it prevented new injuries thereby increasing labor utilization. It wasn't long before the Plant Manager got wind of this so when Frank's boss retired, Frank was a natural for the supervisor's job. Now Frank was in charge. "*This guy has balls*", said the manager, "*we need people with balls.*" Now Frank could **call** many more people slackers and assholes any time he wanted to - directly to their faces! His AQ was rising rapidly but this was fine since his stature was also rising.

Then a new encounter occurred. Frank's boss, Sam Suckhole, an insipid runt of a man, controlled the packing and butchering divisions as well as the slaughter division. One day while Frank was walking through packing, he noticed piles of boxes thrown about between the conveyors. Feeling in a helpful mood he walked over to Bill Blastoff, the packing supervisor and said *"Bill, these boxes are dangerous, you ought to clean them up before someone gets hurt. You should tell those boxers not to make such a mess."*

The comment just didn't get taken in the right context. Frank not only irritated Bill but a few of the boxers heard him so the topic at coffee break was obvious.

"Who the hell is this Franklin Asshole?" they muttered, *"Where does he get off telling us what to do?"* This only gave Bill more fuel for the fire. The next thing that happened was that Frank's boss, Sam Suckhole, called him in the next day to ask about his encounter with the Packing Department. *"Look Frank"*, he said, *"packing is not your concern, so keep your nose out of there unless you are asked!"* Guess what was happening to Frank's AQ? And guess what was happening with Frank's stature on other AQ lists?

Frank was infuriated and steamed back to his office to sketch out a memo to Herbert Hoyle, the Plant Manager. Then he walked into the Plant Manager's office with it. *"Mr. Hoyle,"* he said, *"I have produced a memo to formally identify a terrible inefficiency. To summarize, there are ten points. First, the Packing Department is dumping boxes all over the floor between conveyors. This is a hazard to maintenance as well as workers. They are also producing excessive boxes beyond the packing capacity. This means they may have too many boxers. It also means they are using excessive space which could be used for conveyor expansion. Why not get rid of some of these jerks, save money, be more productive and provide space for expanding the conveyor system? The possibilities of improvement are vast..."*

Herb interrupted Frank, *"Hold on Frank, slow down a minute... let me read your memo and get back to you this afternoon."* Guess what? A meeting was scheduled for the next day, with Frank making a presentation. Bill Blastoff, Sam Suckhole and Herb Hoyle were told to be there, along with the Vice President Earl Klutz who just happened to be visiting Hoyle on a plant tour.

By this time it will be noted that Frank has increased his sphere of influence from a local to a divisional level. Not only that, he was now dealing with middle management, a completely new group of characters. Even Frank's boss was involved in the AQ program. Now he was really cheezed off because Frank had ignored his advice to mind his own business.

At the meeting Frank tried to be cool and he just presented the facts as he saw them. Bill Blastoff and Sam Suckhole were asked to comment on their lack of movement on the issue. While Earl Klutz sat quietly, Bill raged and Sam said it was a good idea,

he just hadn't had the time to activate similar measures.

Well the fact that Sam had just been telling Herb how efficient the boxing operation was didn't help the situation. It didn't take long - the next day in fact, to move Sam into the cattle warehouse as Senior Advisor to the Steer Manure Disposal Task Force. And Frank was promoted to Manager in Sam's place.

Through the next year, there wasn't a mess that Frank didn't catch and raise hell about. Everybody came to know Franklin as he thundered through the plant. He was dedicated to raising his AQ. He wasted no time telling people that sloppy workers were not going to be part of his team.

Herbert Hoyle moved on to head office since there seemed to be so many improvements at the plant. Earl Klutz then made Frank the Plant Manager. Now there weren't many people left to get on the local AQ list. At some point Frank had an encounter with each and every one of the plant people.

He had either **told** them directly they were an Asshole and better shape up, or he had **treated** them like an Asshole. Frank was at the top of the heap. His AQ had risen but his position in the company was also rising.

But the story doesn't stop here. Frank began to meet a new breed of people at the Plant Manager's meetings. He began to encounter the head office breed. By now Frank had become involved in other areas such as administration, finance, marketing and so on - most of which he knew very little about. But that didn't matter to Frank… at least at the plant level. *"Beefs beef and everybody eats,"* he used to say, *"why make a big deal about marketing? An efficient plant is where it's at*!*"*

This attitude eventually got Frank into trouble at a general meeting oriented towards a marketing strategy. Now Frank was rubbing shoulders with the executive level from head office. Frank's new era started at one of the meetings where he was making his usual statements about beef when Slink Wirlwind, the VP of Marketing took exception to the comment. Slink had just given a short presentation

stating that consumer prices were falling at 15%. When Frank made the comment about marketing, Slink immediately asked Frank to present his strategy for a 15% revenue increase next year. Not only did Frank put Slink on his AQ list, but he ended up looking like a bit of a boisterous idiot to the others who chuckled to themselves quietly.

Frank vowed to redeem his prestige and went home quietly - licking his wounds. *"I'll fix that bastard,"* he muttered. *"I'll show the Asshole how to increase revenue!"*

Frank was merciless when it came to cutting costs and keeping people in line. Not surprising, the plant ended up producing a better profit than other plants, despite prices. Frank had no problems pointing this out at all the inter-division meetings, each time modifying his AQ. In the meantime, the plant was creaking with tension. Labor unrest, deteriorating equipment, and new issues were beginning to surface. But so what? Frank was making the company a lot of money.

Through a few more meetings, Frank learned to be careful about what he said. Not only did he pick up some of the executive tricks, he had had a chance to take several courses on tactics, presentations and a course on "The Practice of Hedging on the Futures Market". Finally Frank was invited to a meeting at head office where some discussion was to take place on the crisis of falling prices and the affect on the next year's profits. Frank was ready - he would just wait for Slink to screw up.

About one hour into the meeting, Slink was laying out where future sales would come from. *"We are rapidly moving into an age of meatball mania,"* he said smugly, *"we have done a psychological profile analysis of high school graduates. Conclusively they say that they have just begun to appreciate the importance of meatballs instead of chicken burgers and expect them to play an important part of their lives. Without a shadow of a doubt,"* he grinned with cool arrogance, *"we must direct our marketing energies towards all retail outlets which have any capabilities for distributing meatballs.... all our research and projections indicate a possible unprecedented growth. Perhaps,"* he said, *"you gentlemen have some ideas?"*

This was Frank's queue - he had it in for Slink anyway. *"Mr. Wirlwind"* he said as he stood up, *"we are currently sitting in a situation where falling prices are shrinking profits quickly and where plant and operating efficiencies must play a vital role in securing more profit regardless of price. We have seen during the last year how my plant has, through attention to this basic principle, produced more profit than all others put together. Rather than dream about teenage consumers, we should attend to the reality of the present..."*

Slink was shocked and stood up in anger. *"And what is your miracle plan Mr. Hardass?"* he asked wryly.

Remembering his Commodity Hedging course, Frank said *"One of the most effective means of preserving capital and profits is through the hedging mechanism by clearly selling forward cattle, hogs and pork bellies, then buying back at anticipated lower prices or delivering the commodity which we have at our Ranching Operations. This has the effect of locking in profits even if prices decrease, as you and our VP of Finance, Mr. Dancer knows."* Turning to the President, Frank continued his pitch. *"Thus, in my estimation, we should have the marketing division concerning themselves with anticipated price trends and educating themselves in hedging techniques, rather than doing surveys on meatballs...."*

Frank quite elegantly succeeded in doing several things. He got back at Slink for making him look stupid on plant efficiency. He took a good shot at Slink and his department and positioned himself as superior. And, he brought out a new idea. To top it, he even took a shot at Scab Dancer in Finance. Well, the air was thick with smoke and the silence was frightening as AQ counters clicked away. Finally the president said, *"Frank, how do you propose we can take advantage of this and what is the cost?"* So the meeting shifted focus to Frank and a simple idea. Fortunately for Frank, he had learned to delegate almost anything he knew nothing about, just like the others in the meeting.

He simply went to the board and showed with some simple price changes in one year what the impact would be, depending upon the resulting projections, which he said, must be the responsibility of good market analysts. He said the costs of execution were trivial since all principles, and staff, were already in place.

It didn't take Frank very long to become the Vice President of Operations. Frank had also learned to do something new - he could actually **tell** someone senior he was an Asshole and then **treat** him like one - right out in the open. Now as VP of Operations, Frank dealt directly with new people at a different level. He could now call in all plant managers and tell them they were assholes when profits dropped. He could threaten the new plant manager at the operation that he had almost destroyed through his ferocious and merciless price-cutting... absolving him of any past problems.

Frank worked diligently on his new level of AQ as he moved up the executive ladder. Note that not only was Frank's AQ rising steadily but so was his position in the pyramid. Frank was getting to be so powerful that he could treat people like assholes without even knowing it. He could just send a memo around and reach people he had never met. It would only be a matter of time before Frank would learn to treat everyone like an asshole and win his way to the presidency.

And therein was the grand finale of Frank's climb to the upper echelon. Only when Frank knew that he was also an asshole, and would enter his own AQ list could he really be at the top, with an AQ score of 100.

What is illustrated here is a fairly normal progression through a company. Although Frank climbed all the way, many only climb part of the way. Nevertheless, the climbing process is the same. Even in the case where one "job hops" the process is still the same. An AQ just behaves differently. In any case, Frank moved upward through the three levels, from worker, through management to executive, each time raising his AQ as he went through successive positions.

Each succession had more responsibility (affecting more people) and each time he encountered wider scope (dealing with new people and larger problems). Frank, quite simply, went from the lower reaches (worker) through middle man-management (doers) to the executive (decision makers) as he went through a very systematic metamorphosis up an AQ progression.

At each step, Frank met newer and more influential people in the organization. At each phase he had to impress someone or show results by out-performing something or someone. This was typically done at the expense of the AQ as it rose higher and higher at each encounter. In each step,

Frank could influence more and more people,  effectively treating them like assholes, without even knowing it. Eventually, of course, there would be fewer and fewer people left. Indeed, Frank had moved from the lower reaches as a common worker, through middle management and into the executive echelon of the company by successfully raising his AQ as he climbed.

But there is another major point to this story. If you look at the 20 years it took Frank to ascend, you find that the actual crucial events that made the difference in the climb were quite few and far between. The situations, and the total elapsed time were in fact minute compared to the whole time span. The vast majority of time was spent just doing a job. Sure Frank needed some basic skills, but the bottom line was that he was moved upwards because he kept his AQ in line with his position. Before I explain this, we need to try to quantify this peculiar process.

What Frank did was he climbed his way up AQ Mountain

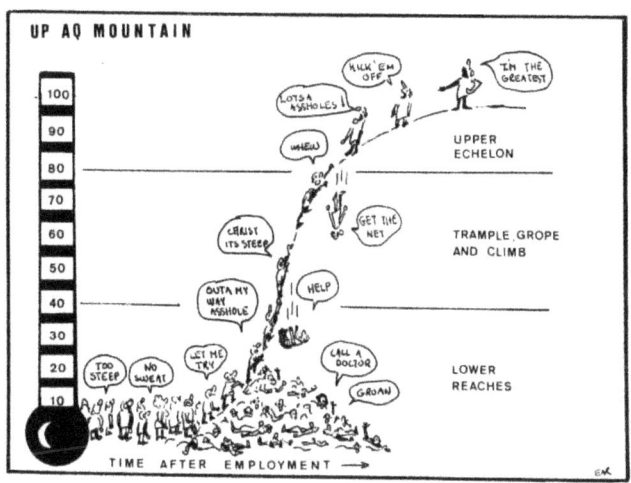

Along the way he picked up some tools to control people and to focus on the bottom line of productivity as an Manager, then profit as an Executive. He picked up some nasty habits of telling people they were assholes and then treating the like asshole. He then went on to become one himself.

3 MEASURING YOUR AQ

We can now consider representing the 5th Law of AQ'ISM as a physical process. The law, which states, "*Individual AQ's have a tendency to rise according to a natural growth process*". The AQ starts low and slow because one takes a bit of time to learn the job and the corporate family. Quite obviously it must end slow because there are fewer and fewer people to convert to assholes. In between, as one's sphere of influence changes, and relations or responsibility increase, the AQ moves quite swiftly. During the middle management time, it is amazing how fast you can make the AQ rise. But the climb gets steeper and harder.

If we can recall Franklin's story, we see that he moved through several phases of stature but if you noted his changing attitude you would notice six AQ phases:

1. he began to **THINK** that some co-workers were assholes
2. he started to **INFER** that others were assholes
3. he gained courage to **CALL** others assholes, at first indirectly
4. he began to **TELL** people that they were assholes
5. he started to **TREAT** people as assholes, most of which was indirect
6. he knew he had to **BE** an asshole himself in order to succeed

Notice how (ironically) you must become an asshole yourself if you are to succeed at the top! This particular sequence, identifying how Frank interacted with others, has a direct correlation with the level of aggression, power, and position. We will identify these as the "AQ METER" phases. The AQ METER identifies the successive transformation process of creating assholes. Regardless of whether you treat, tell, call, infer, or think, the end result is the same - you have created an asshole in some way or other. What is important to the individual's corporate growth is the particular sequence of AQ phases. This metamorphic process from when you first "think asshole" to when you become one must be carried out in careful order - in conjunction with the AQ number.

In following the career path or professional progression of an employee it is obvious that he must move from a potential "nobody", through various supervisory levels, management and possibly into the executive. This will depend upon where the employee enters the company. One of the important ingredients in this progression is related to the AQ-METER and the level that one has achieved. And how does one achieve a new level? Well, here is what it appears to reduce to. One does not usually attain a supervisory role unless he has the "moxy" to **call** someone else an asshole. Right? Or more appropriately convey to his superior that someone or something is wrong, can be improved upon, etc. The transition to Manager, however, requires that one must be able to confront people directly, to **tell** or prove another's unworthiness should disciplinary measures be required.

The next level can only be achieved by being able to **treat** others as assholes if this becomes necessary in the course of duty. Now bear in mind that this does not mean that you always need to be a negative jerk, you just need to show the superiors that you are able to handle conflict by being "tough" if you need to be. The truth is that we all like to be "team players" and "coaches" or "leaders", not jerks. But when the shit hits the fan and all that great team stuff doesn't work, what does management resort to? A team whistle? Hardly. They need to build on their ability to climb up the AQ Meter. It should be noted that the AQ climb upwards normally requires firstly accomplishing each previous phase of thinking, inferring, calling, telling and treating... without skipping any one phase.

If you find this hard to believe, think about a new employee walking around calling people assholes. His career is in immediate danger. Or think about the wimpy manager who is afraid to tell people they are assholes because they were over budget. His career may also be in danger. And how many vice presidents would retain their positions if they were not able to treat people like assholes if they needed to? In fact, one must successively show an ability to work well with one phase before being allowed to activate the next. This process is illustrated as the AQ meter phases in the picture on the next page.

There are three levels to be aware of. In the first level, as a worker, Frank set out to either disagree with or irritate co-workers in his department and even got into trouble with his superiors. His local AQ, if computed on the basis of total department workers, was, needless to say, maximized. In the next segment of his life, when he moved from supervisor to plant manager, and into the middle management category, he had new people to piss-off or disagree with. The situation was a bit different, however, in that he was working at a higher level and could affect more people at one time. In fact Frank could hold a meeting and piss off a whole group at one time simply because he was not happy with something and told them so. Frank's next level occurred when he moved to head office as VP Operations and into the executive level.

Again he could deal with new people and make even wider-reaching decisions. Now Frank could just send a memo to all divisions and treat huge numbers of people like assholes without even seeing them. One memo, if carefully worded by an asshole could effectively get the whole company on the AQ list! In each of the three levels Frank would have a limited number of people to place on his list and therefore he would eventually maximize his AQ in each of the three levels. Since the overall AQ is cumulative, AQ saturation is possible within any one spatial location. That is, if you work in an isolated group there are only so many people you have contact with, even though there are many more people in the company. Conversely, as you move into the executive, there are more and more people you can affect without even knowing them.

So out of this can be created another AQ Law.

9th LAW OF AQ'ISM
Your local AQ will rise to its level maximum within a period of 2 years.

Now this one is odd in that there appears to be an average time period within which an AQ can rise to dangerous levels. This means that if you take work in a particular department or localized group it will take 2 years to get most of the group on your AQ list. Six months to do the job well, six months to figure out what to disagree with, six months to get the courage to change that which you disagree with and six months to reap some benefits. Every step takes its toll on the AQ list. So what do you do when everyone in the group is on your list… including your boss? Well, if you become the boss you may be ok but if you're not, you are in **AQ Disequilibrium** and you may be headed for trouble! The whole process is cumulative and it is difficult to escape it unless you move to a new company.

If you should join a company at a junior level and begin by calling others assholes, you would have missed two steps and could be terminated quite easily. In other words, you would not have conditioned your audience properly by going through the lower steps. Any attempt to miss steps on the ladder can quite easily result in falling off into the lower reaches. The net result could be to get fired or displaced (as Sam Suckhole did) to useless senior positions or to just become a general nobody who could only think, infer or maybe even indirectly call others assholes. These failure cases will be fearful of trying anything higher on the AQ ladder. These people are a special class of workers because they are in "AQ Disequilibrium". This is where the position is lower than the AQ suggests it should be.

We can now create an "AQ METER". This meter tells you what AQ Level you should be at given any particular position. Conversely, knowing what your AQ is should indicate the level and position you should be at. An interesting aside is that you cannot usually jump steps unless you have come into the position from outside. It should then take 2-3 years to reach a state of AQ Equilibrium.

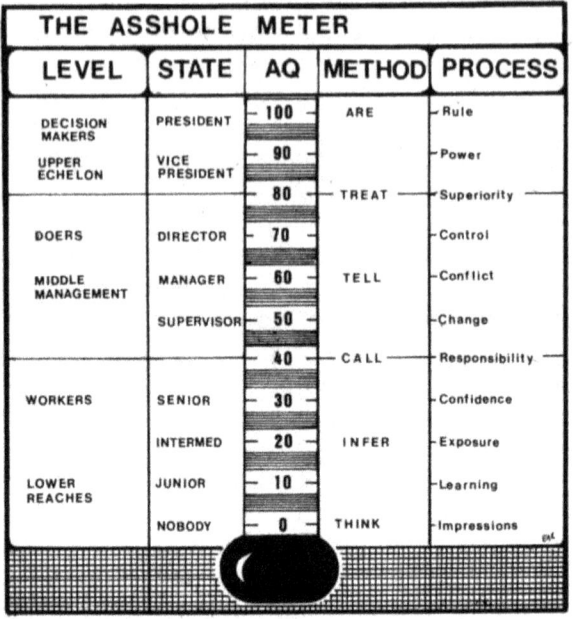

Finally, we have the 10th Law:

10th LAW OF AQ'ISM
Your level of responsibility must rise in direct relationship to your AQ level.

Now, let us find out what happens when you violate some of these equilibrium laws.

4 AQ AND YOUR PRODUCTIVITY

In the previous section we saw how the AQ Meter phases of think, infer, call, tell and treat were key factors in a natural progression into management and executive levels. Thus, there was a direct relationship between the AQ, the phases and the corporate position. A mismatch is known as **AQ Disequilibrium.**

As an AQ reaches higher levels, a very dangerous situation exists when the position in the company is not equally as high. Remember that it is high because you disagree with or don't like someone else and that this is more than likely a reciprocal arrangement. Moreover, it may be high because you have treated others badly, sometimes unknowingly.

Remember also that an asshole, once converted, becomes difficult to convert back. When an AQ reaches great heights, it may become very easy to get fired or laid off, or even receive lateral to lower demotions. Needless to say, if you don't like a lot of people, your dislike cannot be hidden for long and eventually pressure will come to bear upon you, particularly if your position is not lofty enough to allow such prerogatives.

It is at this point that your survival will depend upon your skills, and your position. This will determine your progression (or regression) to a new position. Paradoxically, those who do not make moves to disagree with or do not become forceful with others in an outward manner, will not progress into upper management. Recall how Frank took certain initiatives to create assholes? Are these assholes not your paving stones to progress?

In AQ Equilibrium, as the AQ and position increase, so does productivity. If any mismatching occurs there can be a negative impact on productivity so the converse occurs where efficiency *decreases* as the AQ increases. In this respect, various crisis points are evident along the AQ Meter, particularly at points of transition between management levels. First let me explain productivity.

Quite clearly upon employment, one's time is spent in activities of "learning the ropes" and meeting people, rarely interfering with another's productivity or work habits. Upon learning one's job and being exposed directly to other's work, one can go through a period of increasing his productivity quite substantially.

There comes a time where familiarity of the tasks performed, knowledge of other's work, and exposure to methods will result in some form of criticism, or disagreement that may result in a betterment of production. If the employee does not get his way in such matters he may become disgruntled, lose respect, and, of course, become less productive. Recall Frank's progression?

In further carrying on this scenario, the new ideas and work efficiency will affect the judgment of the employee's competency and promotion. Changes to existing systems usually mean, however, that someone else or someone else's ideas need modification and this can result in considerable conflicts (higher AQ). It then becomes necessary that one must be able to convince or sway others to precipitate a change that will increase production.

Failure results in a lack of promotion and further disgruntlement, thus further lowering productivity. It is at these failure points that AQ and productivity can diverge rapidly. Effectively, one can be busy fighting, convincing, writing, etc., to better things, raising AQ quickly with each encounter, yet spend less time being directly productive. Passing through this phase will be at another's expense and will depend upon the individuals' tenacity in convincing others. That's when you take a swooshing ride down a productivity slide, and your productivity (and possible position) decrease rapidly.

In fact, productivity begins to be measured on the basis of how quickly one can effect change. Eventually the individual will have to gain wider exposure, taking more and more responsibility for a certain function, department, etc. and begin to control people, processes and money directly or indirectly. More and more emphasis is placed upon effective direction, supervision and management of people and production processes.

The next phase depends upon the ability, again, to precipitate change but at a greater or higher level. That is, more and more people/processes are affected and entirely new areas, or methods or projects must be exploited to the good of the company. Anyone who has shown ability to manage people, projects or processes effectively is a candidate for greater things. He must, however, be able to seek out and exploit new and profitable opportunities for the company. This rather idealistic scenario describes the transition of an individual from the workforce through middle management into the executive.

Now what we have described is a **Worker** who has undergone a change into a **Doer** who has changed into a **Decision Maker**. Each transition marks a potential crisis point where very opposite effects can occur in terms of productivity. If failures occur which deny movement from **Worker** to **Middle Management** or into **Executive**, a drastic change in productivity can occur. Needless to say the higher up the AQ METER this occurs, the greater the affect on company productivity and the individual.

As a worker, productivity increases by learning and doing a special task or tasks well, possibly modifying tasks to be more efficient. As a middle manager, productivity increases by better control, direction and motivation of people. This then would create a more efficient process. As an executive, productivity increased by new acquisitions or major changes as related to new or existing opportunities, directions or processes. The evaluation and assessment capability would be highly important to affect production and profits.

As this process continues it should be kept in mind that one is battling the PETER PRINCIPLE and failures along the way become bigger and more devastating to both company and personal confidence. Thus, several major failure points are possible resulting loss of productivity, power and position. These were the productivity slides mentioned earlier.

The effect on personal or company productivity is obvious depending upon where one got to before the slide downwards.

In looking at these failure or crisis points, at the three levels, negative efficiencies are created as:

- More and more time is spent criticizing people or work, bothering others and causing trouble.

- More and more time is required to motivate people, to maintain existing production levels and to convince people of change.
- Criticism, antagonism and subjective emotional meetings are common - resulting in a lack of control.
- More and more time is spent in meetings arguing about opportunities and useless details.
- Personality disputes interfere with decisions that could improve company profits or opportunities.
- Blaming others is common.

High AQ's have a tendency to become more destructive over time. The absolute extremes include a dictatorship with power or a babbling idiot without power. Even worse is a senile old has-been with power. As mentioned before, through the phenomenon of interassholism any company can ultimately achieve a state of ASSHOLE SATURATION where everybody thinks, infers, tells or treats everybody else as assholes. This state becomes fairly evident when employee turnover is slight, giving everybody sufficient time to get to the infer, tell and call levels of the AQ METER but not having enough promotions to go around. The result is failures, disgruntlements, discontent and diminishing productivity. In fact after a few years, people assume seniority and begin to:

- believe that menial tasks are below them
- do just enough to get by until a promotion appears
- believe they are independent thinkers and that the method of doing a job is up to them alone
- believe that they alone are experts
- become protective about their positions and prior decisions
- take more advantage of the company in terms of expenses, liberties

- spend more time in discussions about other's affairs and company politics
- become more concerned about job security than job efficiency

It is easy to see that the above can easily create too many "bosses", poor motivation, lack of control, disorganization and decreasing productivity. Such environments become very depressing as tyrants and powerful imbeciles attempt to control complainers, slackers, and unproductive people with a deluge of ever increasing rules, policies and general administrivia.

The stupidity of the situation is that everybody thinks that they are great and that the other guy is the incompetent asshole. What really happens is that everybody just becomes a bigger asshole to the other guy - but we will examine this in a separate section.

So contrary to normal corporate rules of hiring for long times, minimizing staff turnover, it may be desirable to encourage the opposite, thus avoiding

Asshole Saturation. The whole process, once entrenched, will eventually collapse the company given any economic change. In good times, there is room, profit and potential for all, and saturation continues unattended and unnoticed. But just imagine how productive the situation is in the example above. Like Government?

5 AQ DIS-EQUILIBRIUM

In the previous chapters, we saw how some people rise through positions into more and more power. In reality, the vast majority of corporate citizens remain simply do not rise. As others climb the mountain then fall, their productivities fall. Additionally, through the interassholism effect, they may view each other in ever changing perspectives.

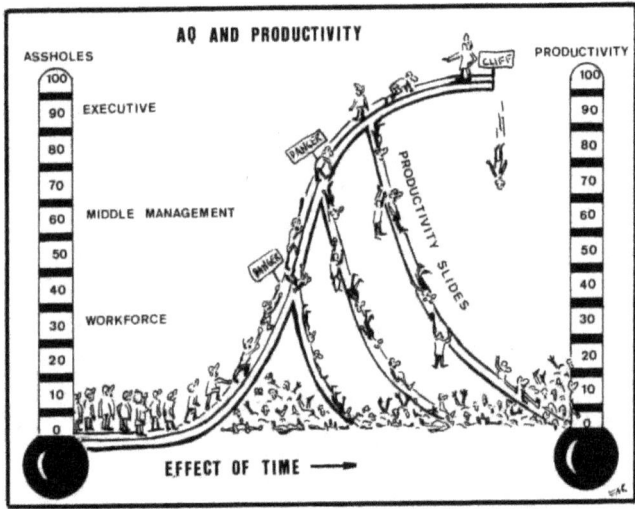

In real life only a select few can climb their way upwards at the same pace as their AQ. There can only be so many supervisors, managers, vice presidents, etc., in any company. But what happens to the others? Obviously they are in AQ DISEQUILIBRIUM! People fall off the AQ ladder constantly but this doesn't drop their AQ - it can even climb faster depending upon how disgruntled one is from the fall. Have you ever seen a happy demoted employee? Or how about one who hasn't been promoted while his co-workers were? What about those who have received poor evaluations and no wage increases? These people think just about everybody is an asshole. Even the guy who got caught feeling up the cleaning lady quickly converted everyone who found out about it.

So despite corporate positions, AQ's still continue to forge ahead, even accelerating when the disequilibrium gap is wide. It has been stated that once a conversion does take place, the process is virtually irreversible. That is, there is such a thing as a corporate memory that doesn't forget, so an asshole once created is an asshole to stay. Yes, I know you can hug and make up but that's not the way the AQ works. What really happens is that people begin to associate various qualities with the assholes. They begin to see each other as bigger and bigger assholes. Consider the following statements:

- You are an asshole!
- You are a big asshole!
- You are a gigantic asshole!
- You are an enormous gaping asshole!
- You are without a doubt the greatest asshole I have seen!
- You are an asshole so incredibly ugly that you defy imagination!
- You are an asshole of such staggering stupidity and ugliness that it can only be matched by your personality!

Have you ever wanted to say any of the above to either your boss or some other little creep who has rubbed you the wrong way? Notice if you would, the strength of conviction in each of the statements. Notice also that certain qualities are being added increasing in size. Even if you can't say it, you can infer or think it! Remember Franklin in the marketing meeting when Slink Wirlwind did a "gotcha" on him? Guess what Franklin would have loved to say? What about the top guys that take a fall and get demoted to lower levels? Some actually stay there but can you imagine how they really feel about the guys who did it to them?

In the corporate culture, all the workers can get converted by each other slowly and methodically into assholes. At this point in time the appearance changes in the eyes of the one who converted him. Suddenly, a picture of the other's posterior is showing through all of his fancy feathers. From now on the appearance gets worse and worse.

That's how it all starts - then at some peculiar point, all corporate qualities disappear and people just look like bigger and bigger assholes. If this could be visualized, you would probably imagine these people as small creatures with ever increasing posteriors, with big feet to hold them up, with small heads and beady eyes, and big snouts to slurp with. Disgusting isn't it? Consider two types of these disgusting creatures and see if you have ever encountered one.

There is a term used, called a **Grunt.** It is simply some useless citizens that lazes around in the corporate mire with little direction or purpose - relatively harmless guys. But **Slinks** are a different group because they unfortunately retain power or influence and can be dangerous. They can trample you, drown you in trivia, turn others against you behind your back and do many devious things to you. Unlike the Grunt, their main purpose is to retain, by any means, their positions, regardless of their capabilities. Slinks are the most unproductive and dangerous species in the corporate culture. You may be able to think of a few who have "fallen from grace" but for some reason are still there. These guys have an agenda to get back up the tree and trample anyone in their way.

Obviously they have learned a few tricks in creating assholes and they would have picked up even more assholes on the way down the productivity slides. So the AQ is in total disequilibrium with their position.

To carry this a bit further, consider there are two types of evil Slinks - those who slurp (Slurper) and those who peck (Pecker). You have probably seen a Slurper type quite often. He is the one who retains his position (above you) by slurping to someone with power. His tactics, well developed, are used to constantly hide his incompetence, or to side with some powerful person who can protect him. The problem is that the incompetence is not usually hidden to those below. The Slurper just becomes one of the most disgusting creatures in the company and is often quite obvious. This little insidious person just loves to blame others to protect or gain position. When these people gain power and authority they can be the most devious people around and they are difficult to dismantle in the corporate structure.

Now the other Slink – the Pecker – is an even more dangerous corporate creature. This one doesn't rely so much on defensive strategies like suckholing (the term used for someone who "sucks" up to others for personal gain). He is trained to use offensive tactics to peck others for survival.

He is the shifty creep who is always seen in your boss's office telling him things about which you cannot defend yourself, and that he can use to his advantage. Unfortunately they, again, have position and power and are totally incompetent.

Ok, perhaps I have exaggerated this a bit, but remember, this is a satire? Enough said about the characters. In the next section we will finally examine where you and your AQ reside in this culture. It is now time to have a look at how to find out what your own AQ is and how you may fit into this new look at corporate structure.

6 SO WHAT'S YOUR AQ?

Are you ready? Now we come to the business of determining your own AQ. The easiest way is to consider yourself as part of a physical group such as a Branch, Head office, Operation, Division, Plant, and so on. This is usually quite clearly indicated by a telephone list or better still, a list of employees and titles in your group. You, as a member of this group, are in one of three levels, mainly the executive, middle management or the working class. First, you must split the list into three groups and count the number of assholes within each group.

GROUP	EXAMPLE
Executive:	Chairman, Vice Chairman, Presidents, Managing Directors, Directors, Vice President, Assistant Vice President, or equivalent titles
Middle Management:	Superintendent, Manager, Treasurer, Controller, Foreman, Chief, Supervisor, or equivalent
Workers:	The rest

In classifying assholes, follow the group guidelines below.

ASSHOLES ARE WORKERS WHO YOU HAVE:
thought, inferred, or called something negative
told off or treated badly
do not like
disagreed with
talked to others about as stupid
consider useless, inferior, incompetent
had to reprimand
reminded of policies, procedures
taken advantage of
treated badly indirectly or directly
bullshitted or lied to
taken things away from

Remember that you must not be forgiving just because the guy was nice today, even after your fierce argument yesterday. This doesn't take him off your list! If you are high up the management ladder, it becomes more difficult to assess or enumerate those you have converted to assholes. This is because it may have been indirect. Remember Franklin Hardass when he sent a memo to all plant employees to cut coffee breaks by 3 minutes? Frank was treating everyone in the plant like assholes, regardless of what he thought he was doing.

	EXECUTIVE	POSITION
√	Boomer Steadfast	Chairman of the Board
√	Franklin Hardass	President and CEO
	Scoot Blastoff	VP Operations
	Flash Spreadsheet	VP Finance & Admin.
√	Slink Wirlwind	VP Planning
	Herbert Hoyle	VP Engineering
√	Angus Steadfast	VP Projects
	Murk Muddler	VP Legal & Corp. Affairs
	4 Assholes of	**8 Total**

So you must think about all those situations where you gave somebody a bad review, had to remind someone about policies or when you sent nasty memos – regardless of reason or justification.

Let us use an example at Steadfast Meats and a list of all the employees. Let's look at Fred Fantasy's AQ at corporate headquarters and put a check mark beside all the executives that qualify.

The corporate offices therefore constitute a physical group within which we will calculate various AQ's. It will be noticed that for the ease of explanation, the list has been split into the three levels. I need to tell you something about this list. In my own corporate travels, I encountered these particular characters so a name has been chosen to reflect that character and I have exaggerated them just a little bit! As you get to learn more about these people, you may even find close similarities to many in your own corporation.

Now here is the Management Group.

	MANAGEMENT	POSITION
	Marcus Mule	Manager Projects
	Fred Fantasy	Manager Planning
√	Randolf Snooper	Director Personnel
	Clepto Superbyte	Dir. Inform Tech
	Micro Tabulate	Chief Accountant
√	Bill Blastoff	Ass. Man. Planning
	Donna Dingdong	Man. Marketing
	Grunt Hollowhead	Sup. Projects
√	Pomp Crotchley	Sup. Personnel
	Oscar Ostrich	Controller
√	Kevin Baloney	Sup. Ind. Relations
√	Prim Strutland	Sup. Admin. Services
√	Willy Liplock	Assist. Man. Operations
	Cut Thrasher	Sup. Systems & Operns

	Gross Fartley	Man. corporate Affairs
√	Barf Chapstick	Man. Legal
	Slime Mealymouth	Sup. Mech. Engineering
√	Horace LaPrick	Sup. Ranch Operations
	Clone Mimicker	Sup. Ind. Engineering
√	Switcho Stumpbrain	Manager Engineering
√	Wimp Wishwash	Sup. Support Services
10 Assholes of		**21 Total**

And finally, here are all the guys that do the work.

	WORKERS	**POSITION**
√	Gayle Grimley	Acc. Payables Clerk
	Moose Baxter	Special Serv. Coord.
√	Hump Pussywhip	Sr. Financial
√	Feelo Ballsack	Jr. Draftsman
	Buff Windbag	Sr. Financial Analyst
√	Cirilla Gorilla	Sr. Systems Analyst
	Sleeze Huffer	Sr. Engineer
	Quirk Multiples	Systems Analyst
	Fanny Bumwiggle	Secretary – Legal
√	Lardo Billobum	Solicitor
√	Irk Guffer	Accountant
√	Lila Memomangler	Legal Clerk
	Dork Assgrabber	Intermediate Draftsman
√	Sam LeSlam	Project Account
	Oink Freaker	Administrative Assistant
√	Slip Goofball	Special Project Engineer
	Jaybird Warpmatter	Engineer
	Lou Kabbagetop	Sr. Planning Advisor
	Viola Broadbum	Int. Mechanical Engineer
	Bula Bugle	Business Analyst
	Spasmo Mover	Industrial Engineer
√	Korno Klutz	Engineer
	Vera Sparkle	Receptionist
	Dudley Dwarfbrain	Marketing Analyst
	Fats Gutstuffer	Computer Operator
	Birtha Bitchalot	Sr Filing Clerk

	Name	Title
✓	Jock Flasher	Supply Clerk
	Souse Growler	Int. Mech. Engineer
	Tina Tinkle	Operator
	Polly Perfect	Personnel Assistant
✓	Wormley Crawler	Jr. Engineer
	Slim Twinkle	Designer
✓	Bang Loudmouth	Systems Analyst
	Karen Klutz	Secretary – Eng.
	Dink Primrose	Sr. Accountant
✓	Moira Mouthpeice	Executive Secretary
	Flirt Shameless	Coordi. Office Services
	Wendy Worker	Filing Clerk
	Olga Titwhopper	Executive Secretary
	Buzz Bottle	Int. Planner
	Calc Theorem	Marketing Engineer
✓	Marf Garfle	Accounting Clerk
	Grog Stinky	Engineer – Planning
✓	Harvey Hotshit	Planner
✓	Barry Brass	Int. Engineer
	Blam Featherflash	Marketing Analyst
	Warp Monkeynuts	Programmer
	Milo Muff	Support Person
	Suzy Bubbles	Accounting Secretary
✓	Dork McPork	Coordinator Ranching
	Perky Shortwhip	Sr. Advisor
✓	Bark Banana	Legal Assistant
✓	Wino Dingbat	Business Analyst
✓	Rolly Growl	Budget Coordinator
	Nose Grindstone	Jr Designer
	Crass Farkle	Project Engineer
✓	Moon Flasher	Engineer – Design
	Milly De Dilly	Secretary
	Brenda Breeder	Personnel Clerk
	Piles Bumrubber	Designer
✓	Herf Honker	Solicitor
	Ruff Honker	Jr. Programmer
	Garfle Greymatter	Systems R&D
✓	Whipply Grizzlepuss	Draftsman

✓	Sac Meddler	Personnel Clerk
✓	Grim Rectum	Planner
✓	Jerk Jerkins	Eng. – Mechanical
	Tina Droop	Executive Secretary
✓	Marcus Mule	Financial Analyst
	Rhonda Grinder	Secretary
	Eric von Shithead	Industrial Rel. Clerk
28 Assholes of 71 Total		

First, you must place a check mark beside each one on the list whom you classify as an asshole (as per the previous guidelines at the start of the chapter). You may have already noticed that I have marked some... this is Fred Fantasy's AQ calculation. You need to do this for each group and find how many assholes you marked out of the total for the group.

For example, Fred thinks that 4 of the 8 executives are assholes. When Fred goes through the management list, he marks down 10 of the 21 Management people. Then when he goes through the worker list, he comes up with 28 assholes in a group of 71. Now he can take these numbers and place them on a summary tabulation to calculate the percentage of assholes. Fred has a BASIC AQ of 42% (total assholes/total employees).

GROUP or LEVEL	NUMBER ASSHOLES	GROUP TOTAL
Executive	4	8
Middle Man.	10	21
Workers	28	71
TOTALS	**42**	**100**
	BASIC AQ	**42%**

Now this BASIC AQ in its simple form is a pretty good indication of your AQ level, particularly if the company is small. The trouble is that you may work for a huge corporation and therefore your AQ may appear insignificant overall, yet the local AQ or the group that you work with may reflect a high AQ. Obviously, the local AQ is more relevant so you need to use the people in the corporation that are local to you. As you gain a higher status in the company, there is a need to expand your list, but normally, the physical location of the groups dictates. The other aspect is that there are certain key modifiers of the AQ. For this reason, you can use the more technical method to modify your Basic AQ. Here is how you do this.

You must weight each group by a ratio. This means looking at each group individually and calculating your RAW AQ for each group. Then you multiply each RAW AQ by a predetermined weight (taken from the AQ METER). The total of the result will be your "RAW AQ". Go through each group and calculate Raw AQ.

GROUP or LEVEL	NUMBER ASSHOLES	GROUP TOTAL	PERCENT ASSHOLES
Executive	4	8	50
Middle Man	10	21	48
Workers	28	71	39

Now you can use the weights against the results, as follows:

GROUP or LEVEL	PERCENT ASSHOLES	WEIGHT	RAW AQ
Executive	50	x .20	10
Middle Man	48	x .40	19
Workers	39	x .40	16
		TOTAL RAW AQ	45

The next procedure involves modifying the Raw AQ depending upon how many of your *line supervisors* are on your AQ list. The reason for modifying the

AQ in this manner is to consider the impact your immediate bosses can play if anyone of them are on your list. Needless to say, if <u>your</u> boss is on your AQ list, then you could be on shaky ground. If <u>his</u> boss is also on the list then you may be on dangerous ground. If the <u>next</u> boss is also on your list then you may indeed be living in a very precarious corporate world... unless your position is such that you are able to displace one of these guys. In order to bring your position back into line with your AQ, you should be contemplating moving out before they send you down one of the productivity slides. It should go without saying that your most immediate supervisors are the ones who can most affect your corporate growth and attitude. Your immediate boss, therefore, will damage you or your AQ the most. For this reason we must compute the AQ modifier by giving less weight to the asshole boss who is further away. This we call the "LINE AQ".

Your (Fred's) Boss	.25	.25
His Boss	.15	.15
Next Boss up	.10	.10
TOTAL MODIFIER		**.50**

For example, let's look at Fred again. Fred is the Manager of Planning and has his boss Slink Wirlwind ticked off, plus Slink's boss Franklin <u>and</u> the Chairman Boomer! So here is how Fred would modify his Raw AQ.

Total Possible AQ	**100**
less RAW AQ	**45**
EQUALS LEFTOVER AQ	**55**

Fred must tick off which of the three supervisors up his supervisory line are on his list. He therefore ticks off all three modifiers in the little table, adds these up and gets a total of .50 as the modifier as you can see. If Fred had only his immediate boss classified as an asshole he would only have .25 as the modifier.

Now we must multiply this number times the "LEFTOVER AQ". Leftover AQ is simply 100 less your Raw AQ as calculated previously. Finally, there is one more step to get to your real AQ. Your real AQ is the total of your Raw AQ plus the Modifier times the Left Over AQ. Note that the Modifier times the Left Over AQ is the "Line AQ". Thus your real AQ, is the total of your RAW AQ and your LINE AQ.

LEFT OVER AQ	times	MODIFIER	equals	LINE AQ
55	X	.5	=	27
			PLUS RAW AQ	45
			EQUALS YOUR AQ	72

In Fred's case he would get 72. He would add a whopping 27 points to his RAW AQ of 45 because he has all three line supervisors on his list. Now just think about that for a minute. If you thought all of your line supervisors were assholes, would you not think that you were on dangerous ground?

Now that we know how to calculate an AQ, let us examine its relation to the AQ Meter. Once you have determined your AQ, you can then look at where you are on the meter. The next page shows the AQ Meter with the related positions. It also shows you how to calculate your AQ on the same sheet… shouldn't you have one of these pasted on the wall of your office?

For example, if your AQ is 42, then you should be at a supervisory level. If you are just at a junior position, with an AQ of 42, then you are in AQ-DISEQUILIBRIUM. If you are in such a situation then this is a signal that you may be in trouble. If, on the other hand, your AQ is lower than your position warrants, this is ok but you may not be able to progress beyond a certain point in the climb upwards. This means that at some point you may have to treat people like Assholes and this may go against your nature - the reason an AQ may be too low.

Let's get back to Fred Fantasy. Fred ended up with an AQ of 72. On the AQ Meter, this means that Fred should be ready for a Director position. This is not so good for Fred as he is still a manager so he is in AQ Disequilibrium. The fact that he has his line supervisors on his AQ list is good, but he needs to start thinking about telling people they are assholes directly. As a manager, he can only call people assholes. He wants to take this opportunity with a few people to assert himself so he can impress those line supervisors and get promoted.

Here's a summary picture for you.

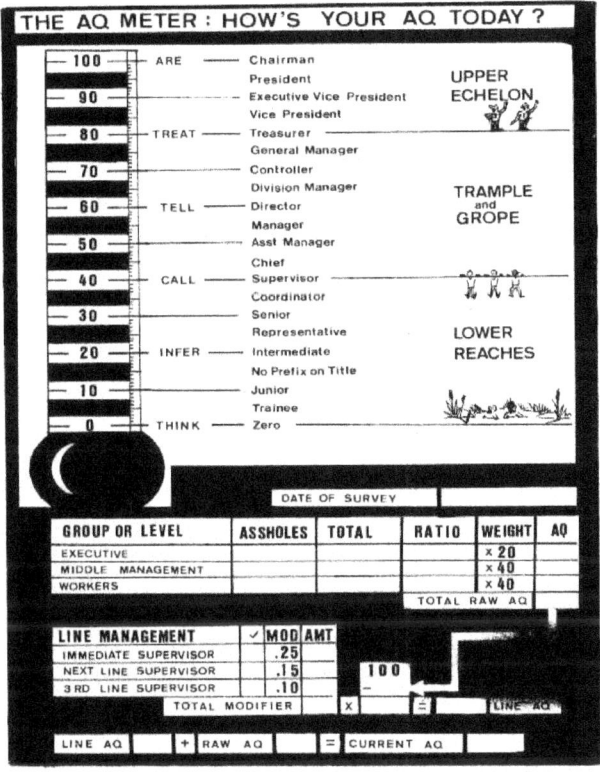

7 SOME AQ EXAMPLES

Ok, we now know how to calculate an AQ. But what does it mean? Well, let us take four examples from Steadfast Meats and get to meet some characters plus get a look at their AQ's. We will examine the AQ meter in detail and see how this can apply to us. Are you ready for this?

CASE 1: SCOOTER BLASTOFF

Scooter is the Vice President of Operations. He is part of the Upper Echelon. In his quest upwards, Scooter has had to learn how to tell many people that they are assholes. This was hardly difficult for Scoot because he was a pretty big one himself... although he never thought so. Much of this he has accomplished by using his favorite expression that he is becoming "disappointed in the performance." The fact is that Scooter delegates things so fast in such a deluge that it is difficult for anyone to maintain consistent performance. Just recently, Scooter learned that it was much more effective to treat people as assholes directly - "be direct," he says, "pressure shakes the loose turds out of the sack pretty fast – it's the sticky ones you want anyways - who wants to waste time motivating dumb bunnies and assholes?" It was this attitude that allowed Scooter to move into the executive, simply because he ceased to look like and be "one of the boys".

If we look at Scooter's RAW AQ, we find that it is fairly high (75). This is because, as pointed out,

Scooter shows less and less tolerance for slackers and low producers. "They wouldn't get away with that kind of shit if they worked for me!" he would say. Now Scooter reports to Franklin Hardass and his next line manager is Boomer Steadfast, the owner and chairman. "Boomer," he says, "is just a senile old fart and Hardass is the big asshole in the company!" This means that Scooter's LINE AQ is 10. (Modifier of .40 times LEFT OVER AQ of 25). The total AQ is 85, which seems high, but if we look at the AQ METER, we see that he is in AQ Equilibrium - situation normal.

In this case, the fact that Scooter has both of his line management on his AQ list is even ok. This is because he has already learned how to treat people as assholes and because his disagreement with his boss gives him the motive necessary to attempt displacing him. But let us suppose that Scooter was only an Operations Manager (i.e. one step down) with the same AQ of 85. Our meter shows that he is allowed 75 and obviously he would be in AQ Dis-Equilibrium.

In fact, he could have three line supervisors on his list and his AQ could be higher. In this case, his position would not support an AQ of 85, and with his bosses on his list, he could well be on precarious ground. But why would Scooter be in AQ Disequilibrium? He may not have been deemed as executive material. He may not have learned to treat people as assholes for the good of the company. He may have been too obvious about his feelings to his superiors. And so on. In any case, the danger signals would be obvious.

CASE 2: OSCAR OSTRICH

Oscar is the Controller so he belongs to the middle management group. Very much unlike Scooter, Oscar is quiet and seemingly cool. The fact of the matter is that Oscar really doesn't like conflicts and he certainly doesn't like to discipline anyone. So Oscar tries to avoid conflicts, ignores chaos, and spends a lot of time either doing the work himself, keeping his head buried in the sand, or quietly grumbling in his office. Being quite sensitive, Oscar has, over a few short years, devastated his AQ. He has just kept adding to his list by thinking that others were assholes. Just recently, because of frustrations, he has begun to infer and call others assholes - but never directly.

So when we add up Oscar's AQ, we find it sits at 60. We also find that Oscar's boss, Scab Dancer is on the list as is Franklin Hardass who is Scab Dancer's boss. Boomer Steadfast, who is the 3rd line supervisor is not on Oscar's list yet because he has not had much to do with him. Oscar doesn't like his boss much because he is "two-faced" and "makes stupid irrational decisions". "Franklin Hardass," he says, "just never seems to listen". This brings Oscar's AQ up to 76, well above what his position can support, so Oscar is in AQ-Disequilibrium.

Oscar is currently caught in a terrible dilemma - he doesn't particularly want to call people assholes and he certainly doesn't like to tell people they are assholes, and far be it to actually treat them like assholes. But his boss keeps telling him: "Oscar, you can't go anywhere without moxy." Oscar's productivity is also suffering since he spends more and more time mumbling to himself - adding assholes to his list. It is just a question of time before Oscar takes a trip down a productivity slide if something isn't done. So far, Oscar's boss tolerates the situation because Oscar is a competent accountant and a nice guy, but as Scab puts it: "I am getting tired of solving some of your problems, Oscar - we are not pleased with your performance".

CASE 3: ERIC VON SHITHEAD

Eric is in the working class, working as an Industrial Relations Clerk. Eric reports to Kevin Balony who then reports to Scab Dancer. Eric's greatest problem is that he is simply not a very nice human. His personality, like a torn boot, is ragged and dirty. He would be classed as a Super Slurper, hardly adding to his credibility. Eric keeps his job by making sure that he takes care of his boss's every whim, and everyone knows it.

Eric just doesn't get along with too may people since he believes he is the smartest guy around and just can't wait to tell everybody - regardless of where and when - how important industrial relations is to the company. Nobody likes to listen to Eric anymore and some even tell him to "piss off and bother someone else". Others can be seen accelerating their walks by his office to avoid him seeing them. It is hard for Eric to understand this since he thinks he is so smart and company conscious.

Within a very short three years, Eric has tallied up a fairly impressive AQ. While various superiors have even told Eric to "cool it", others have told him to "piss off". Others try to ignore him - without attempting to hide their actions - the end result is to lift Eric's AQ. With a RAW AQ of 50 and the two line superiors above his boss on the list, Eric has a total AQ of 63. Now this may not seem like much, but Eric is only allowed an AQ of around 20 - very dangerous indeed - particularly at such a junior level. Eric has certainly learned how to *tell* and *call* but his position does not allow him these luxuries - remember the jumping of AQ Phases? No, no, no…

it just can't be done. So Eric is also in Dis Equilibrium. Worst of all, he hasn't used the phases of infer, tell, call, etc. in step with his rising AQ to attain the equivalent position.

In fact, only Eric's boss, Kevin Balony is willing to stand up for him. This saves Eric from being fired since Kevin insists that Eric does good work and is a devoted company man. The fact is that Kevin likes to have the creep catering to him. The situation, however, is quite precarious in that the day Eric gets on Kevin's AQ list could indeed be the day a change rapidly occurs.

CASE 4: DONNA DINGDONG

Donna is the Manager of Marketing, residing in the Middle Management Class. Donna reports to Slink Wirlwind who reports to Franklin Hardass. Donna, quite clearly, is just a happy worker as she flits about dreaming up projects. Donna has only been there a year, having been hired by Slink for her credentials. Donna was a Professor of Economics, with virtually no practical experience. So Donna has had little time to develop her AQ. She has only had a few bad experiences, mostly chauvinistic encounters, so her RAW AQ sits at about 10. Franklin Hardass, the president, however, has made her list, so her line AQ adds another 14 points. Her total AQ of 24 is still well below what her position allows (mainly 55) as a department manager.

Being lower than the allowed equilibrium AQ is not yet a problem with Donna. It will become a problem, however, if she is required to utilize the AQ Phases which support that position, or she raises her AQ above that allowed for her position. What will happen is that she will not be able to come across as aggressive, put people in their place, threaten them, or change rules. This will do the opposite of Oscar and Eric, and allow others to take advantage of her. The AQ disequilibrium will work against her because she is just wrapped up in a nice little world, not paying attention to those clods and sods who <u>are</u> paying attention to their AQ's.

Now, you may think these people are silly, but I can tell you I have known them and they are not exaggerations. When you examine people, they all have little secrets, idiosyncrasies and may have great corporate power over others.

We now come to see the delicate balance between one's AQ, one's position and how one creates corporate assholes. We have studied the AQ and we have seen what it means. We have also seen how to monitor it as a measure of one's corporate progress and cultural health. Next, we will look more closely at some special corporate characters and their main avenue of direct communication - the meeting. Let us find out their secrets in dealing with the AQ.

8 THE EXECUTIVES

So what now you say? So we can measure our AQ. What's the big deal? The big deal is that we can all learn from these laws and perhaps avoid becoming too big an asshole ourselves? Perhaps here is a way of monitoring your progress in a corporation that sends up some warning flags about how you are feeling about others, your level of job satisfaction, and how you are treating others?

Obviously you can measure your AQ to detect dis Equilibrium, but there is something else we can learn here. If we look at the experts on how they manage this phenomenon – control it to their advantage, it is usually the Executives who are the best teachers. Let me explain.

THE BUSINESS OF MEETINGS

The corporate meeting is an extremely interesting mechanism. It is one of the most convenient ways of assembling, disseminating, exchanging and evaluating information quickly - at least in principle. Meetings, it seems, like our corporate citizens, become more and more regimented and predictable as we move higher up the corporate pyramid. Indeed, if handled properly, meetings can be effective ways of conducting corporate business. And yet it is the one mechanism that most everyone has to learn from scratch and by experience. For example, the power of meetings and the power of writing corporate "memos" cannot be under emphasized as necessary instruments to corporate growth. It is odd that these are not taught in school - the exception possibly being a Business College. Most professionals must learn to write and how to conduct themselves at meetings on their own initiative - before they can rise.

Meetings are the place where each can assess the other - it is the place where "men are made or destroyed". It is here that everyone is at the same elevation as opposed to sitting in the tree at his or her relative statures. Here they can look good or foolish depending upon how they have learned the meeting/memo game. This becomes more and more important as one moves higher up the ladder. In fact, one's professional ability in the area of original training (i.e. Engineering, Science, etc.) becomes less and less important. The training or educational degree just becomes a paper credential with little depth to it. Executives will always tell you that:

1. They do not have time for details since that is what the support staff is hired to take care of...
2. The bottom line and the cost benefit analyses are the key factors...
3. They have a long list of technical and management experience...
4. They are not yet convinced of the merit of your proposal.

There are four main reasons for this attitude. First, they usually remember very little about their training because they either forgot it or it is outdated. Secondly, corporations are essentially financial animals and they must be able to think and behave in financial dogma. Thirdly, they spend so much time in meetings, listening to problems and proposals, that they have no time for anything else. Fourthly, meetings are a good way of avoiding a formal commitment – i.e. discuss it instead and see what the others think first. Well, of course this may be a cop-out to hide their lack of knowledge, but on the other hand, they have picked up a new knowledge, which the technologists have yet to learn - Meeting Technology! This knowledge must be gained with the rise in AQ.

It is in this aspect that meetings bare their prime purposes, for they show everyone who matters how any individual can handle both presentation and evaluation aspects to the "good of the company". That is, how does he evaluate, manage or do what he is responsible for? In any company, therefore, it is wise to pay attention to this aspect.

Thus we have the **LAWS OF ADVANCEMENT:**

LAW 1: Law of Progress
You will progress only when you "do your job well".

LAW 2: Law of Competency
Your "job competency" will be judged by someone above you.

LAW 3: Law of Valuation
You must "convince" someone above you that you are doing well.

Well, if you dare to venture into this arena, the meeting is the quickest way to progress. This is where you can "show off" to those above you. This is called exposure.

You can show that you do your job well and you can convince others besides your boss that you have great potential. On the other hand, it could be a quick way of proving to those above you that you are a real twit.

Meetings, it seems, always have "judges" in attendance. They will attempt to evaluate presentations and performance. Since the meeting's function is to deal with information, it will also be judged. The quick way to stardom is to get these judges together and put on a performance. A couple of good performances can even put pressure to bear on your own boss - if you so desire.

It should be noted that certain items in the LAWS OF ADVANCEMENT are in quotes. These deal with your "competency" and the act of "convincing" someone of your competency. When one considers that, according to the PETER PRINCIPLE, each has a tendency to rise to his own level of incompetence, it makes a mockery of the competence judging process.

Secondly, how one convinces these incompetent people is also quite a joke, particularly if one tries to relate this to his technical ability. In conjunction with the LAWS OF AQ'ISM, we find that because corporate people constantly seek profit, power and prestige, meetings become great gatherings of corporate assholes that meet to "jockey" for position. Everyone attempts to impress someone else, regardless of whether someone else is an asshole. And, because companies exist to produce and make profits, it follows that the best way of impressing superiors is to convince them that you can get things done in a better or more efficient way - convince them that you can affect the bottom line of time and money.

Consider that there are three types of meetings (Executive, Management, Supervisory levels) that provide analyze, then evaluate information successively. Each group becomes less concerned with details because they were closer to their levels of incompetence. Thus you begin to seriously question how companies survive.

But this is the game you must play. Let us sum up with a new **LAW OF MEETINGS** as we approach the Executive levels:

> Meetings bring together a group of incompetent assholes who attempt to exchange and present ever-deteriorating information in such a way as to impress each other so they can become bigger assholes and affect company profits.

Sounds quite horrible doesn't it? Well, actually if one could sit outside meetings and watch the proceedings, one would indeed see quite a show, particularly at higher levels where AQ's are fairly high. Think about the number of corporate failures every year. Do you think this asshole phenomenon has anything to do with it? The funniest meetings are where INTER-ASSHOLISM has taken its toll and ASSHOLE SATURATION is evident. Let us examine meetings in more detail.

WHAT'S THE BIG DEAL ABOUT MEETINGS?

You may ask at this point: "So what? What is the big deal about these executives and their decision making meetings?" The big deal is simply that this is where the big deals are made, by little fellows like you and me. The other big deal is that these fellows don't really know much about the details on which they are making decisions. In fact, the more detailed they try to convey, the stupider they look. That's why they are after the "bottom line".

Now this Law of Meetings is a fairly strong statement but if you have ever watched an executive meeting, you should see the logic. Just think about your own meetings and see if there is any similarity. Another big deal is that these executives spend more than half of their corporate life in these meetings where they make decisions on things they appear to know little about. Do you think, given the amount of time spent in meetings that they have developed a toolbox of their favorite tools? Do you think these may have anything to do with their AQ's and keeping them healthy?

SO WHAT'S THE SECRETS?

If we look more closely at the meeting, we see that Franklin Hardass had the power. Not only had he the power of the president but he also had the power to maintain order and control. So which comes first - presidency or ability to maintain order? We see that the attendees certainly had a few things in common.

- They had some formal education
- They had, in their climb upwards, managed to get through each of the bottom two levels by some special accomplishment
- They have worked a long time so they are fairly senior
- Their AQ's are fairly high so they don't mind being assholes

But these common items in no way answer why these big assholes are in control. Having an education is no big accomplishment and working a long time is hardly significant. We see that these fellows are just the same as anybody else, with little peculiar habits and tastes, with idiosyncrasies and incompetence's like any other corporate member. In fact, if you could take an executive's power and clothing away he would look like and behave like any other "normal person". Well clothing can be bought but what of this power? There are two other items left on the list - getting through the levels and their AQ's. Somehow the acquisition and retention of power must be related to these two items.

We have seen that one's height in the corporate tree seems to be proportional to his AQ, so to be an executive it is best to attain a correspondingly high AQ. If not, you may not be able to treat people as assholes so as to properly climb upon them. In addition the way in which one climbed through the AQ phases was critical - keeping the AQ and position in equilibrium. By paying attention to these two aspects, somehow power and height was attained. But before we examine more closely this process of getting power, let us look again at corporate environments.

THE CORPORATE PLAYGROUND/BATTLEGROUND?

There is always a thick interplay between boardroom characters. Typically details are skimmed over rapidly except where a more general topic is tabled. You will note that much of the hard-line basis to the questions was bottom line based... the profit motive. More important, there is a constant jockeying for "one-upmanship" positioning as each one works quite diligently on his AQ levels. It is easy to see that no one has any reservation when the opportunity comes to treat the other members like assholes - no reservations at all!

Obviously, if this is really the case, then the best way to be successful is to accept the fact that you will be an asshole and work away at being the best (asshole that is!). But not all people believe that climbing up the ladder is a success measurement, nor do all wish to be an asshole. On the contrary, some people would prefer to keep away from the ladder altogether.

Others may want to achieve a certain height and then just do a good satisfying job. But whatever your choice is, it must be realized that the very nature of a corporation generates competition for positions, success, money and power. It therefore becomes difficult to simply sit quietly and not be involved. You cannot sit in isolated oblivion while those above are constantly watching you for better production or mistakes, while those below are after your position.

Whatever the case, power of some sort must be learned and used. Similar to playing a football game, you must first learn the game rules. Power, in the corporate game, is different in that nobody willingly tells you the rules of the game! So while your AQ rises, you are forced to play by learning the rules through trial and error - fairly dangerous to say the least! And if one of the rules is that you must become an asshole, then it is not surprising to see many people fail to play the corporate control game very well. If we look at people in a company, we could group them into four types:

Type 1 Climbers - they want to climb to the top.
Type 2 Plateauers - they want to climb to a level and stay.
Type 3 Cavers - want to be left alone.
Type 4 Grunts - don't give a shit either way.

These four types make up the players on the corporate playground, each with varying levels of skill and knowledge of the power game rules. For those who do not play well, the playground clearly becomes a battleground for power as those who learn the rules will trample the other poor slobs. Most professional people work to better themselves in a company.

This means position and power or status and money, so they are immediate entries to the battleground. With the exception of Type 4 Grunts, these players must learn both offensive and defensive techniques if they are to reach their objectives. So the Climbers must know both defensive and offensive rules well, while the Cavers need to know defensive techniques. The Plateauers need offensive rules to attain the desired level - then they need to know good defensive rules to maintain their status. If you don't believe this then just consider the following statement:

All people in a corporation are there to be nice to each other all the time. They all try to give each other help in getting more money and they all work in harmony to make the company a lot of profit - so they can share it. Seniority is determined solely by the number of years in the company because this is directly related to intelligence and productivity...

Is this absolute unadulterated horseshit or isn't it? Maybe the following is more applicable:

All people in a corporation are trying to take advantage of each other so that the company makes money. The idea is to minimize the help to the other guy so he doesn't get powerful enough to screw you or take away your money. Anyone who shows any sign of weakness is trampled and crippled. At regular intervals groups will get together to hold a trample contest, seniority being the reward for standing at the top of the heap. This way the company has the fittest people at the top...

Is this the way it is or is this just crap as well? How about this scenario:

The people who are at the top of the company are there because they are smarter and superior to the others who work for them. Order is accomplished by a loyalty to the company that in turn ensures productivity. People work to better the company and to ensure that the smarter ones are assured more money. Because the top people are so smart it is normal that they choose the smartest ones from below them as their successors...

More bullshit, right? What about this:

All people in companies are motivated by profit, power, prestige or some combination thereof. These are derived directly by being responsible for the improvement or betterment of the company, as assessed by someone in a more senior position. Order, control and efficiency are accomplished through a hierarchy of power and authority systems that are based upon management techniques. Those who learn the techniques well will be more likely to affect productivity and attain the spotlight needed for assessment. The one's who learn and use these techniques the best are the ones most able to rise to the top...

Is this closer to the truth?

Although we have cited some fairly wild extremes, the truth probably lies in a combination of the four scenarios. Whatever the case, may be, the scenario is like a playing field with the attainment or retention of power being the goal. So what are these rules? Let us first examine the playing field.

We have already looked at the executive playfield. It was called the BOARDROOM. This was where we saw the executives use their skills and apply the game rules - to the best of their abilities. And because the executives represent the elite highest order in a company, it goes without saying that they should know the rules best. Right? After all these are the people with the most power and they make the most significant decisions. Moreover, they make the most money, and their chosen means are MEETINGS. Why? IDEALISTICALLY meetings provide the following:

- They are the most effective way to accomplish many tasks.
- They are the best way to communicate information to others.
- They provide a necessary face-to-face interaction.
- They provide the means of developing collective solutions.
- They create the feeling of being part of a team.
- They can develop a sense of joint commitment.

This is what meetings are <u>supposed</u> to provide! As the executives tell you. "Meetings are an intensive way of involving others in solving problems and making decisions which can improve the company or its people. Involving others in problems or decisions is the most effective way to ensure that they will accept and support the results." That's the way it should work - and in many cases it does work this way. But we have a strange paradox associated with the business of meetings.

Meetings are everywhere, taking up significant time, effort and money. It is estimated that if you are a middle manager you will spend 35% of your working time in meetings. By the time you are an executive, this percentage will have reached upwards of 50%. That is a significant amount of time! The strange paradox is that even though meetings take up such an incredible amount of time, the technology of insuring that meetings are indeed effective is given little importance.

What this means is that the key rules to be learned in the boardroom meetings are not taught, but learned through experience - possibly by trial and error. And yet these rules, which obviously give one effectiveness and control in meetings, must be one of the key ingredients to the attainment of power. The clues to these rules are in the executive meeting. Here we can see the executives joust and jockey for positions, power, money and status. This is where they deal with all those difficult decisions, don't they?

At any rate, the whole point of the chapter is to identify the idea that corporate meetings and their players constitute a very significant segment of any company. In addition, we can undoubtedly pick up the most pointers on how to play the corporate game by looking at those who play the game the most and those who have scored the most power goals - the executives. They have obviously had the best chance to develop their skills to the highest level wouldn't you think?

THE CORPORATE EXECUTIVE

Let us take a quick look at the corporate executive - that pillar of strength, power and perseverance. He is the great asshole that all those pyramid climbers try so hard to mimic and replace. Or is he or she? It is time to look more closely at this super being's secrets to success – at least the way I have seen it work! Understand that I do not want to pick on the executive as I have lived there myself but... it is pretty clear that an executive represents the group that has best succeeded in the other's eyes. If there are special secrets, then these are the ones to scrutinize. In particular, it is time to have a closer look at what got them there... and what keeps some there. I know these guys and gals use AQ tactics. And what are those tactics? Well it is all about using tools to keep your AQ in line with your position. It is also about changing positions as quickly as is possible when disequilibrium threatens.

As we look deeply into many of the successful executive's behavior, we will see that most of the time they really are the assholes that they try so hard to be and that they use special tools to help keep the status. Somewhere and somehow the executive acquires special weapons of combat that allow them to survive and prosper in the corporate arena. What they do is develop a special set of verbal and tactical weaponry to keep their position in line with AQ.

Let me illustrate this process. Let us say that you are a blooming executive and that you have an AQ that is too low. As you spend most of your executive life in meetings, you can use this venue for adjusting your AQ. You can create assholes by using simple statements. Suppose new staff is invited in to make a presentation. When they finish, tell them you don't quite get how it benefits the company and they need to make a better presentation on the key benefits. That creates a few assholes and you get on their list too. But note that there appears to be a more lofty motive in your little attack. It is for the good of the company, not for AQ alignment, right?

Now consider the other situation where your AQ is higher than your position. Guess what needs to be done here? You need to raise your position... or you could end up a victim yourself, ending up on one of those slides down the productivity curve. Well, the same tactic as above would work if your superiors were there. They would think you were a great corporate citizen and maybe promote you.

Suppose you want to get the AQ up really fast and can't be bothered waiting to get a few assholes at a time? Why not send a memo around recommending some cuts in budgets? That's sure to get a bunch.

Finally, suppose you can't change your AQ alignments at all? Well, I have seen many take advantage of this as well. Take this as your AQ signal to move on... leave to a new job. Take a hint and get out while things look good so you can get decent referrals. Impress the seniors, and then get out. Otherwise you could be on the slide down before you know it.

I know this is a simplified example but I have observed hundreds of common tactics like these that executives like to use. There is a complete untaught technology here on how to handle yourself with your mouth – and with the AQ. If you observe these guys in action, it may become obvious what you need to do to be like those great executives you may admire - so you can also make a disgraceful climb to glory. Maybe working like a dog is the hard way to climb. Maybe paying attention to your AQ is a lot faster... and easier? I certainly don't want to support being a super asshole to get ahead but how many know they are one? Don't forget now, this book is a satire – this means picking fun at all these lofty executives!

If we should look back into the profiles of real climbers they pay attention to what? You guessed it - PROFIT and THE BOTTOM LINE! Not exactly a surprising conclusion, is it? I have yet to meet a successful executive (I said successful, not nice or smart) that did not know about profit and the bottom line. In a high level meeting, did you notice that good executives were always focused on finance – the bottom line – as it is commonly referred to (budgets, profits, revenues, etc.), and those things that affect it (efficiency, cost benefits)? This is the new "technology" for the executive.

Another clue is in various tactics that they learn. The reality is that these are really not taught in school at all… guess you knew that all the time! The reality is that these executives did learn some tricks from somewhere. They are picked up as extra "tactics" that were needed to deal with and to move through the **"Time of the great transition"** that I will explain shortly. What is particularly interesting about this process is that I have observed these same tactics in boardrooms around the world, whether it is in government, Fortune 500 companies or even the smallest company. If we look closer, in fact, we would see that the ones who have progressed the fastest have learned the most effective tricks.

There is a time in every executive's life where he is groomed, or grooms himself for the title of executive. The ones who get here and stay here appear to have learned a very effective set of tools that I call weapons… through that third level of training. If you have ever been in a room with some of these experts, they can cut you to ribbons and make a fool out of you or your presentation in an instant. For this reason, I call this weaponry the **Executive Arsenal**. You may wonder why I choose to call these an arsenal. Two reasons: They truly are weapons used to disarm, immobilize or injure and I guess we may as well keep focused on that human posterior again... the arse as it is commonly referred to.

THE GREAT TRANSITION

At some point in one's corporate life, if one is to climb upwards into the upper echelon, fly with eagles, sit high up in the tree; one must go through the Great Transition - sort of like a corporate menopause. This happens somewhere in the middle management phase when one has to start letting go of that which he has learned and been trained for - to become immersed more in the methods of business and management. Towards the end of this period, he must also develop his arsenal in preparation for the move into the upper management and executive echelon. If he fails, then the process will be difficult and perhaps even disastrous. The Great Transition involves getting your degree in the second and third levels of training.

If I could possibly summarize the Great Transition, it would probably be that period of time where there is an urgent need to understand and adapt to dealing well with "Boardroom Brawling". I say this because executives spend more and more time in meetings... the boardroom... that is where they jockey for position, power and recognition. If you were to spend most of your time in meetings, it would make sense to gather up a new expertise in performing well at meetings. Clearly, some must be weapons that allow one to survive in the boardroom - that place where executives spend the majority of time. Clearly you can't use your technical skills any more so what can you do when AQ Disequilibrium knocks on your door? My contention is that the majority of the Executive Arsenal is therefore made up of weapons used in boardroom brawling so as to adjust that AQ. It turns out that there are actually six arsenals executives use.

These are the secret tools that keep AQ's high. They will be dealt with in detail later. Now we have a new profile of the top executive.

- They usually have forgotten the discipline they used to get the position.
- They have picked some business related education or experience.
- They have developed boardroom brawling techniques.
- They have picked up "bottom line" savvy.
- They have learned to treat people like assholes.
- They are not shy about successfully telling people they are assholes!
- They made it through the Big Transition into management.
- They have somehow successfully come through the Great Transition.
- They have a very high AQ.

Because an executive has moved into a world where boardroom brawling and the use of this arsenal takes up a majority of his time, this distinguishes them from the pyramid below. But they have usually elevated the AQ through the AQ phases of calling, treating and telling so they are good at it. This means that they can treat others like assholes and get away with it as part of normal function. It is this aspect that one must pay attention to. The executive arsenals are just the tools that allow the executive to stay in AQ Equilibrium.

And this little aspect is one of the most significant secrets that executives learn... the art of AQ Equilibrium using the arsenals. How do they do it? Well these tools are very effective in creating assholes so if you need to get the AQ higher to maintain your position, use the tools. If, on the other hand, you find your AQ is too high and you need to elevate your position, try using tools to make yourself look good... at the expense of creating or maintaining assholes. And where is this best accomplished? In the boardroom or in meetings of course!

BOARDROOM BRAWLING

One final word about the most popular AQ training ground... the meeting or the boardroom. It is pretty clear that the executive spends a lot of time in meetings. Estimates vary but this time can be around 60%. That is why the meeting is the true place of performance for an executive. This is the prime battlefield.

I can also tell you that there are many executives appearing on this battlefield who do not know how to align their AQ's... and have not learned the arsenals very well. In reality, things don't always happen smoothly in meetings and many are quite a joke, but if there is an executive present who is skilled in AQ Arsenals, he will surely be the one to watch. Some executives are quite aggressive, and in many cases, self-centered individuals with appetites for power and an insatiable appetite for ego food. Others are just plain stupid. It is not uncommon to see some fairly volatile performances occur when there is a possibility of others threatening a position.

It must be remembered that the vast majority of executives did not get to their position in the tree by just sitting there and doing nothing. And it must be also remembered that these people are constantly being threatened by newer executives lower down who are themselves similar in aggression and needs... and with their own arsenals. They had to replace someone or they had to be better than someone else. So these boardroom meeting places are truly places where great performances (funny or sad) take place.

It has been suggested that meetings are a means of accomplishing critical things fast. We listed several main purposes. It has also been stated that executives are decision makers. This means that they must get to the heart of things fast and make effective decisions on spending money, resolving problems and making profit for the company.

Well, if it worked this way all the time, it would indeed be an efficient corporate world. The truth of the matter is, however, that many executives are not well trained and meetings do not work efficiently all the time. As I said before, the reality is that they do not have much of a clue about technology... or the area of expertise in which they may have started. That makes it a new scene for all. What's the substitute "technology"? Why the "bottom line", "cost benefits", "budgets", "efficiency", "revenues", "commitments", right? It is this that forms the basis of meetings and if you don't believe this, then my advice is to keep away from this group. But I have noted another interesting phenomenon at these meetings that makes it easy to apply AQ tools effectively. I call this the Laws of Executive Regression.

THE LAWS OF EXECUTIVE REGRESSION

It is not hard to understand how many executives become outdated and helpless. Most have forgotten their chosen technology... called a **has-been**.

They also require a new area of expertise, called finance... that makes them **dummies**. Does this mean **has-been dummies** are running companies? Think back to the big meeting we had at Steadfast Meats. Is it surprising, in view of this to understand why the following laws are in force at an executive meeting?

LAW 1
Information deteriorates as it moves upwards in a pyramid.

LAW 2
Meetings bring together a group of incompetent assholes who attempt to exchange and present ever deteriorating information in such a way as to impress each other so they can become bigger assholes and affect company profit.

LAW 3
The more general or simple the topic is, the more likely it is that it will get blown out of proportion.

LAW 4
Authorization is quickly given when the authorizers cannot be held responsible should the project fail and when all of them can claim credit should it succeed.

LAW 5
The greater the cost of putting a plan into operation the less the chance there is of abandoning the plan - even if it becomes irrelevant.

LAW 6
The higher the level of prestige accorded the people behind the plan, the lesser the chance of abandoning it.

LAW 7
Rationality will prevail only when all other possibilities have been exhausted.

LAW 8
The more distant the participants are from the facts the more likely they are to believe what they hear.

LAW 9
The amount of time spent on detailed discussions can be inversely proportional to the financial commitment.

LAW 10
If a majority of the attendees are responsible for a miscalculation no one will be at fault.

LAW 11
Justification procedures will become more difficult as the cost decreases.

Is this silly? Think about it. Can you better understand why so many meetings are such a joke? These are the laws commonly working against progress and these are the laws that help AQ's rise quickly. It is this mixture of idealistic approaches and regressive obstacles with which we see executives functioning. This is the corporate playground where the rules are learned and executed by has-been dummies. But alas, these executives have new skills. I call these the Six Executive Arsenals.

THE SIX EXECUTIVE ARSENALS

Ok, now I have to tell you what these tactics are. I call these arsenals because they are truly weapons executives use and they are so consistently applied internationally I would swear executives have a secret rulebook that comes to them in a flash of light when they attain the title! I have classified them into six major groups, many of which were used in the meeting in a previous chapter. The arsenals are the ways by which you create assholes rapidly so as to re-align your AQ or impress someone in order to change your position.

Arsenal 1 is the **Offensive Arsenal** used to attack an opponent.
Arsenal 2 is the **Defensive Arsenal** and covers the weapons needed to create a defense against the offensive weapons.
Arsenal 3 is the **Aversive Arsenal** used as offensive or defensive methods. They are there to round out the arsenal.
Arsenal 4 is the **Trouble Makers Arsenal.** It is designed to deal with people who need to be put in their place
Arsenal 5 is the **Cultural Arsenal** and it includes methods outside the boardroom to also align position
Arsenal 6 is the **Manipulators Arsenal**. It is used to get your way.

These are the tactics that Executives use. If you really want to know what they are and have a good chuckle of how silly – and yet effective – they are, you can get these in my more detailed book, *"Corporations stripped Naked 1: Exposing the AQ Virus"* and *"Corporations stripped Naked 2:*

Controlling The AQ Virus" If you are itching to see the scores of tactics these fellows use and see the funny and not so funny methods, you should find some laughs here – and maybe some tips too?

So do I suggest that you use these to climb the corporate ladders? Hardly! But I do suggest you pay attention to your AQ because AQ Dis-Equilibrium is not exactly my idea of a great job or following your passion. It is your thermometer to tell you to change your attitude or move somewhere else.

Accepting these laws as an underlying process is not such a bad thing. You can get a chuckle out of it, and you can work it to your advantage. Simply build your own arsenals of immunity to the virus and monitor your AQ level. Remember the Peter Principle? It reflects the fact that you become further and further removed from what you knew best… you become incompetent! Sorry but that's reality. The AQ tools are how Executives, and many other defeat this problem and avoiding those devastating productivity slides downward in position and stature.

Here is the bottom line. If these laws are working against you and your AQ is in Disequilibrium, you have three key choices:

1. Raise your AQ to be in line with your position.
2. Raise your position to be in line with your AQ.
3. Leave and zero out your AQ.
4. Refuse to fall victim to the AQ Virus

Arsenals are used to make 1 and 2 happen as quickly as possible, and the executive, who spends so much time in meetings, has become expert in developing this new expertise. You can learn from them and laugh about it too once you see this AQ process clearly.

So ends our satire on corporate life. Hopefully this summary has given you a new perspective on corporations and those pillars of strength at the top. Yes, they were all stripped naked for a while to give you a new look at them. Yes, this was presented as a satire, but in reality I have presented many people and situations that may be more real than we care to admit. In reading all this, you may have wondered what was real and what was fiction. But from now on, at the end of each working day, after all those dealings with your co-workers, just think about a simple question: "**How's your AQ today?**"

But here is the true bottom line: **Don't be an Asshole!**

Ed Rychkun

Check out the full version of this book on www.edrychkun.com and also on Amazon.com

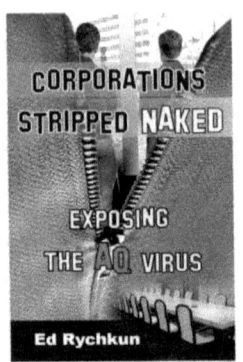

Corporations Stripped Naked: Exposing the AQ Virus
Take a tour of corporate life through former business executive Ed Rychkun's view of his lifetime of climbing corporate ladders. This provocative and hilarious expose' shows what really goes on behind those boardroom walls. It reveals the flip side of a company's naked underbelly by showing how people universally conform to laws on how they feel about each other called AQ'ISM – a classification of "Asshole". Using his own 30 years of climbing ladders to the top, he exposes how top management falls victim to a viral cross between the Peter Principle and the IQ. Using large Fortune 500 companies, as well as smaller enterprises as his stage, Ed relates his first hand experience in maintaining positions of Managers, VP, CEO, Founder, Director, and Chairman.

Ed examines the social behavior of corporate citizens and develops his universal laws about how this feeling is quantified as an AQ, and how it can have a direct impact on how fast you can climb or fall from the corporate ladder. Ed tells it like it is, revealing how the "real" professionals - the Executives, use a set of secret AQ Arsenals to hide their incompetence and maintain their positions of power in the corporate hierarchy by making asses of others. You will immediately recognize a similarity with your own situation and derive humor from it. But beware, as one critic points out, *"Never was the raw naked truth so aptly expressed as in this earthy examination of the blatantly exposed underbelly of the modern corporation".*

In this sequel to **Corporations Stripped Naked: Exposing the AQ Virus**, Author and former business executive Ed Rychkun brings new light into the Law of Attraction as he takes you deeper into the naked corporation's secret tactical AQ arsenals. He strips companies naked of their professionalism and glamour to bare the Executive and Management tools of power and control that gravitate into a darker side of the AQ virus and a universal phenomenon he dubs the AQ. Using his own 30 years of climbing ladder to the top, he exposes how top management falls victim to a viral cross between the Peter Principle and the IQ. Using large Fortune 500 companies, as well as smaller enterprises as his stage, Ed relates his first hand experience in maintaining positions of Manager, VP, CEO, Founder, Director, and Chairman. Find out what really takes place behind closed boardroom doors. Get a new perspective on a naked corporation as Ed reveals what the real experts, the Executives and the Managers, use as universal tactics and tricks called the AQ Arsenals to hide their incompetence and climb the corporate ladders fast; and to maintain order and control. See how you can monitor your progress and avoid the AQ Virus of moving to the dark side of corporate life. Get fresh look on how to avoid and control this virus by utilizing to your advantage the Laws of Cause & Effect, and the Law of Attraction.

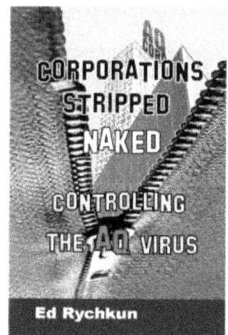

www.ingramcontent.com/pod-product-compliance
Lightning Source LLC
Chambersburg PA
CBHW071154090426
42736CB00012B/2331